The Other Side of the Door:
the art of compassion in policing

Rachel Parish and Jack J. Cambria

Published by DRI Press, an imprint of the
Dispute Resolution Institute at Mitchell Hamline School of Law

Dispute Resolution Institute
Mitchell Hamline School of Law
875 Summit Ave, St Paul, MN 55105
Tel. (651) 695-7676
© 2020 DRI Press. All rights reserved.
Printed in the United States of America.
Library of Congress Control Number: 2019907778
ISBN 978-0-9827946-8-5

Mitchell Hamline School of Law in Saint Paul, Minnesota has been educating lawyers for more than 100 years yet remains committed to innovation to respond to the changing legal market. Featuring more enrollment options than any law school in the country, Mitchell Hamline is committed to accessibility and offers a curriculum rich in advocacy and problem solving. The law school's Dispute Resolution Institute, consistently ranked in the top five dispute resolution programs by U.S. News & World Report, offers more than 30 alternative dispute resolution courses each year in a wide variety of domestic and international programs, including certificate programs in arbitration law and practice, problem solving, and conflict resolution, and is the home of DRI Press. For information on other DRI Press publications, visit http://open.mitchellhamline.edu/dri_press/

About the Authors

Rachel Parish is an artist, cultural producer, and community organizer. She works nationally in the US and the UK with a focus on social practice and creating new performance for stage and public spaces. Recent productions include *Museum of Our Forgotten Selves* (Cambridge/Coventry, UK), *Throw Me on the Burnpile and Light Me Up and Be Here Now* (Aurora Theatre, Atlanta), *Revolt. She Said. Revolt Again* (7Stages, Atlanta), *Opera in the Shower* (Works on Water, NYC and Art on the Beltline, Atlanta), and *The Drum Major Project* (city-wide, Atlanta).

In Atlanta, Rachel works as Artistic Director of the *Little Five Arts Alive* Creative Placemaking initiative and serves on the Charting Board of the Little Five Points Alliance. In the UK she is collaborating with arts and research partners to develop an interactive audio-adventure animating the inner life of infants for adult audiences. Recent Artist-in-Residencies include at Duke University (where she conducted a year-long exploration of the multifaceted role of Failure in society, culminating in an interactive outdoor installation) and at CUNY's Dispute Resolution Center. With this book, she completes the multi-year project at the heart of the CUNY residency, where she worked with members of New York Police Department's Hostage Negotiation Team and Poetic Theater in NYC to develop an experimental arts-based empathy-training course for police officers.

Jack Cambria is a recently retired member of the New York City Police Department who served for 34 years and received numerous awards for bravery and dedicated service. For 16 years he served first as Police Officer, then Sergeant, and then Lieutenant in the Emergency Service Unit (ESU), which provides Rescue, SWAT, and Counter-Terrorism services to the City of New York. He has served on many high-profile assignments such as both World Trade Center disasters, plane crashes, and a variety of hostage and barricade situations, particularly those involving violent and suicidal individuals.

In 2001 Jack was assigned to command the agency's elite Hostage Negotiation Team, coordinating the efforts of over 100 negotiators who respond throughout New York City. For fourteen years he was responsible for the training and certification of all new negotiators and refresher training of all of the current members of the team. Jack is a New York State Certified Police Instructor and has conducted in-service training for many International, Federal, State and Local Law Enforcement agencies, including at the U.S. Military Base at Guantanamo Bay, Cuba.

Jack has also served as a technical consultant in the entertainment industry, providing proper police policy and procedure for major motion pictures and television series. Jack has recently served on the National Police Foundation's committee reviewing the Pulse Nightclub mass shooting incident in Orlando, and is a contributing writer of the on-line published report. He currently teaches hostage negotiation, de-escalation strategies and active shooter presentations for law enforcement and corporate entities across the country and internationally, and he has authored several scholarly articles on negotiations. Jack received his Master's Degree in Criminal Justice from the John Jay College of Criminal Justice – City University of New York, where he has also taught as an adjunct professor.

Contributors:

Maurice Emerson Decaul is a member of New York's Poetic Theater.
Chris Honeyman is a dispute resolution consultant, mediator and arbitrator based in Washington, DC. He has directed an almost thirty-year succession of negotiation and medi-

ation research-and-development projects of national or international scale (www.convenor.com/projects).

Elizabeth Jeglic, Ph.D. is Professor of Psychology at John Jay College of Criminal Justice, City University of New York. She has helped to train new members of the NYPD Hostage Negotiation Team as well as police recruits.

Teniece Divya Johnson is a writer, yoga instructor, Intimacy Coordinator for film and stage, and professional Stunt Performer, cultivating self healing and safe mental health practices to empower dangerously authentic storytelling.

James O'Shea, MD is Assistant Professor in the Department of Emergency Medicine, Emory University, Atlanta, GA, and the department's Interim Director of Postgraduate Medical Education. He is based at Grady Memorial Hospital, the busiest trauma center in the Southeast U.S.

Jenny Pacanowski is a member of New York's Poetic Theater.

Daniel L. Shapiro, Ph.D. is Associate Professor of Psychology at Harvard Medical School, and founder and director of the Harvard International Negotiation Program. His most recent book is *Negotiating the Nonnegotiable: How to Resolve Your Most Emotionally Charged Conflicts* (Penguin 2017.)

Maria R. Volpe, Ph.D. is Professor of Sociology, director of the Dispute Resolution Program, and director of the CUNY Dispute Resolution Center at John Jay College of Criminal Justice, City University of New York. She has helped to train new members of the NYPD Hostage Negotiation Team over many years.

Georgia Winters, Ph.D. obtained her degree in Clinical Psychology at John Jay College of Criminal Justice, City University of New York. As of Fall 2019 she is an Assistant Professor in the Department of Psychology, Fairleigh Dickinson University

Cover: design, Rachel Parish; photos, Engin Akyurt for Pexels (silhoutte), Jack Finnigan on Unsplash (police officer), and Michael Gaida on Pixabay (barbed wire.)

This book is dedicated to Detective Lydia Martinez.
The authors and contributors thank
the Daniel and Joanna S. Rose Fund
for making the project possible.

Contents

Prologue

Chris Honeyman and Maria R. Volpe

Five New York poets, two psychologists, one emergency-room physician, one sociologist, one Washington-based consultant, one London-based theater director, and last but not least, the chief hostage negotiator of the New York City Police Department: This was the team built for an unprecedented project, and not by accident. The team's composition is at least as attention-grabbing as "man bites dog" — the journalist's classic example of a good story. And the journalist's six classic questions present themselves immediately, of course: who, what, when, where, how and why?

The "what" has been the work of the entire group, from our very different perspectives. The "how", of course, is the core of the book, by its central contributors, artist Rachel Parish and longtime NYPD chief hostage negotiator Jack Cambria. The when and where, meanwhile, are simply stated: The discussions and experiments that led to this book took place from late 2012 to mid-2015, and were centered at and around John Jay College of Criminal Justice, City University of New York, in midtown Manhattan.

The authors of this Prologue, however, are uniquely positioned to set the scene, and to answer the "who" and "why" questions. On the "who": Unusual as the combination of talents offered here may be, we have worked together in different subsets many times before. Chris and Maria, as veterans with decades of experience in the study and practice of negotiation and related fields, have worked together over enough projects and decades that neither of us can remember how the collaborations started. Maria and Chris have worked with Jack for almost two decades, and Maria has worked with the NYPD's Hostage Negotiation Team as a group for much longer. Rachel has worked with Chris for nine years, on multiple projects, and with artists in New York on many more. And so on. The group is diverse, but also (and in a quite New York way) connected on multiple levels.

And now, the "why": This too exists on more than one plane. On a personal level, we were shocked by the death of NYPD Detective Lydia Martinez, whom we saw as the sort of police officer that other police officers might wisely strive to become. We shared a strong motivation to honor Lydia's life by helping to create some small contribution to the possibility of training more police officers to think like Lydia in the future.

On a larger scale, our field, imbued with typical Western thinking, has mostly accepted an apparent dichotomy between art and science. The proposition that there is science underlying many of the precepts, emotions, techniques and effects of art has only recently begun to be the subject of serious scholarship. But there is now a growing body of such research. Discoveries in the last 20 years about the brain, and particularly in the area of neurolinguistic programming, have established that the dichotomy is a false one (see Alexander and LeBaron 2017 / LeBaron and Alexander 2017, and research cited therein; LeBaron, MacLeod and Acland 2013, and research cited therein; Jendresen 2017; O'Shea 2017.) Much of this research and writing has even emerged, as with the works just cited, since the project described here began; we have been pleased, but also a little surprised, at the pace with which (some of) our admitted guesses have acquired scholarly backing.

Yet we remain aware that what this team has created is an experiment, with the usual combination of successes and failures. It is worth emphasizing that we expect as much learning to arise from the things that did not work as from the things which did. This too relates to a concurrent line of inquiry being pursued by one of our team members. Through residencies at Duke University, the Shop Front Theatre in Coventry, and East15 in Essex, Rachel developed a project known as the International Failure Institute. This project directly engages professionals in articulating their failures, arguing that the failures provide some of the best insight into understanding both interpersonal and intrapersonal communication. Frequently, if studied, these failures can lead to new, forward-thinking approaches to solving seemingly intractable problems. Indeed, in this area, negotiation and its related fields could stand to pay even more attention to the sciences, which have long known this and have pursued its logic vigorously.

We hope this book honors the concept. And with that, it's time to turn the subject over to the core members of the team. We welcome their spirit of innovation and risk-taking, as they add to the long-established field of police science what might be argued to be a whole new field. Perhaps it might be called "police arts."

In The Meantime

Maurice Emerson Decaul

The gods looking down from safety
resume their dispute about humans

the interventionists argue for decisive
but limited action

fire   plague, while the peaceniks
remind the others of Diomedes

stabbing Aphrodite, Diomedes piercing
Ares with his spear

the hubris of man. The peaceniks throw
up their hands

let man kill man his blood is his blood,
they argue what is it to us

if he destroys himself & Zeus meant to
speak up

but the debate had moved on to topics
of importance

while below him, people marched &
fought & declared their lives mattered.

$\mathcal{CB} \mid \mathcal{BO}$

On the First Day

Rachel Parish

This project began with a suicide.

Among the different kinds of events that fall within the purview of the New York City Police Department's Hostage Negotiation Team (HNT) are the high profile hostage events you see on TV, with gunmen barricaded at a bank or in a public building. Also included but often less "newsworthy" are domestic hostage situations and attempted suicides: the team considers these to be individuals taking themselves hostage.

However, the suicide problem that I was confronted with on the first day of my collaboration with Jack Cambria, the longtime head of the team, was not one that the team had to try to defuse, but one that had recently taken place within the team's own ranks.

Lydia Martinez was a police detective held in high esteem by all of her colleagues, and was often described to me as someone who was a pure empath, who could create a personal connection with people from all walks of life on the turn of a dime. She will be described at the end of this book by Dan Shapiro, who knew her. But her death was the incident that eventually brought such diverse people to the table to begin this project, not only because it was a tragedy that had affected every member of the HNT on a personal as well as a professional level, but also because it highlighted the simultaneously bold yet fragile power of one of the most progressive approaches to policing and police training that exists in our nation today.

We began, though, without a specific project. Jack and I were simply put together "on spec," from a hunch on the part of Chris Honeyman, a conflict management consultant and a mutual collaborator of Jack and myself. I have a personal background in using creativity for addressing crisis, and a professional background in complex collaboration; Jack had a professional interest in finding a new way of approaching the issues within his field; Chris had an interest in seeing how the two of us might bring the intersection of our work to the wider police force. We had no roadmap and no direct sanction from the department, so the approaches we employed, as well as the understanding of what we were trying to do, changed over time.

The only way to begin was to listen as widely and as openly as possible. And so I listened to story after story, and we tried out different ways of articulating the underlying question of the project. First one out was: *How can police officers learn emotional competence as a policing tool and cope with the fallout of doing so?* This was a solid start. As more context emerged about the particularities of the Hostage Negotiation Team and its position within the larger landscape of police departments, both in New York and across the United States, the question developed to include: *What do we do with the power and the pitfalls of failure and vulnerability in these high-stakes situations?*

The information that continued to clarify the questions emerged in personal, winding and beautiful narrative form. Here are some distilled bits of information that I found particularly useful:

> *The Hostage Negotiation Team's motto is, talk to me.*

> *They are the only unit within the NYPD that calls themselves a team.*

They are a hand-picked group of individuals who all have over a decade with the department, and, most important, have been chosen for their ability to recognize and use their own fallibility in a crisis situation.

The only way to make a connection with someone on the other side of the door, in the HNT's terms, is for the negotiator to be able to connect through their own experience of failure — to be able to say "You know what, I've been there, I know about that, and I can talk to you about it. I can see, from my own life experience, that I could be in your shoes, but I can also see that there is another way." Not "I know what you're going through," because you don't. But rather, "I've been in a bad way myself, and I can tell you about it."

The very best negotiators have access to their own real-life experience of adversity, and are able not only to share the coping strategies they have developed over the years but the humility to stand as a one-time peer to a person in a crisis situation, as someone who has faced a breaking point but who managed to find another way.

Being a selected member of the team is also a volunteer position — these officers hold full time positions in other units within the department — units in which using vulnerability is not a respected approach, much less a tactic.

As my learning deepened, also increasing were the reported number of high profile cases of police violence against people of color. Part of the response to this included demands for sensitivity training for police officers. This functioned to further clarify issues at the heart of our own collaboration. The training and policing tactics of the HNT actually do model the qualities that many people yearn for their police force to use. The fact that this training exists, and is proven and highly successful, and yet exists only in an extremely narrow portion of our police force, causes problems not just for those without access to the training, but also for the negotiators themselves. Having to cope with a work environment that "silos" the best of policing tactics is deeply challenging and can be damaging. Our ideal-world intention for the project had emerged: *Can we help to create a whole police department that operates from a place of compassion and caretaking as a first principle?* And the method: *Can we put my experience in socially engaged art together with Jack's expertise in policing and police training to address this problem?* To be clear, we did not think we would achieve this. But what we had done was to finally say and envision what it was that we wanted to work together toward.

The first phase included my working as an embedded artist with HNT members in trainings and on the job, drawing out stories from them that they would normally not have the opportunity to talk about in an on-the-job setting. The second phase involved formal lectures from Jack and me for police officers in continuing education. The third phase, where the expanding collaboration included a psychological study, was a voluntary series of six experiential learning sessions, for a diverse group of interested individuals, mostly involved in law enforcement in an active or prospective capacity.

The purpose of this third phase was to develop and implement a pilot program, designed to increase emotional competence in current and prospective law enforcement officers. Working with Chris Honeyman and Dr. Maria R. Volpe, Director of the Dispute Resolution Center at John Jay College of Criminal Justice, CUNY, we identified goals for the program and developed six experiential sessions for participants.

Through a combination of activities, we engaged their thinking about policing and the individuals involved in policing in new, active, and personal ways. Our toolkit included mindfulness practices, theatre-based practices including character study and scene analysis, writing and performance exercises with poets, personal and public ethnography the participants conducted in the field, and presentations of case studies from the fields of policing and emergency medicine (to offer comparisons of ways of dealing with compassion in a crisis).

We used ambiguity and cognitive overload as pedagogical tactics. Participants in the workshop were never told what they were supposed to learn or indeed who they were supposed to learn it from. They were never told what they were being taught or where the course was headed. They came up with the key learning points *themselves* through reflection on the exercises. And although this ambiguity sometimes was frustrating to them, they kept coming back for more. And in the fifth session when they found themselves at an impasse, wondering aloud about how to traverse the gulf between an individual's perception and socially situated perspectives — and then when, through holding long periods of silence and frustration, they articulated and expanded upon the possibility of compassion as a key to traversing this gulf, coming up with the words themselves — I felt a little win.

Our ideal-world goal in this three-year project was to create an emotionally accessible police department. Instead we ended up with a three year process of encounters, stories, shared meals, a collection of poems, an interdisciplinary curriculum, a psychological study, and more. We didn't know where we were going to end up. We let the process guide the project. We aimed for the impossible, and we listened, we accepted, and we adapted as we went along.

Forever a Student of Life

Teniece Divya Johnson

Stuck in our ways
Leaves us trapped in a maze
of our own making
Unaware of what lies
outside the black lines
Self prescribed
and/or self defined
Colorblind to a world of possibility
Sinking in a quagmire
of gray tones and shades

No I'd rather be
Forever a student of Life
Yes, forever a student of Life

Learning for self edification
Gives self and
Communal
Liberation
Free from the bounds of misinterpretation

A need exists to serve
the diversity of people
A need for knowledge is key
unlocking the flow
Making it possible
for all of us to breathe
With peace of mind
Trust, respect
Free from the bounds of misinterpretation
A sense of ease
Yes I'd rather be
Forever a student of Life
Yes, forever a student of Life

⚝ || ⚝

Moving Our Metaphors

Much as you might expect in a play, the active voice in this book often shifts. Yet as discussed in Chapter VIII, after extensive discussion the group agreed to define the pilot project described here as fundamentally an arts project. The experimental workshop was then organized using collaborative theatre-making techniques and principles. So the majority of this book is written in Rachel's voice, the "I" you will often see below (except where otherwise indicated), and the core will be a description of the curriculum of the final six-week experiential learning project.

We focus on that phase of the collaboration as it is itself a summary investigation of what the entire process taught us. Interspersed amongst the sections are poems that arose from the six-week workshop, either from law-enforcement participants, or from a group of performance poets who are members of Poetic Theater in NYC and who were themselves collaborators in the project. These poems reflect on both the content and the concepts that arose throughout this collaboration.

Most of this book is a compilation of critical reflection and planned session content. The intention is to take the reader through a practical, informative and reflective journey that somewhat parallels our own. The lessons we expect to learn along the way are never as bold as the ones that arise unexpectedly. The two main concepts that arose through this combination of planned content and ongoing critical reflection are the need to shift our metaphor for policing, and the impossibility of ever putting yourself in someone else's shoes.

In order to start unpacking these two concepts a little bit, I want to tell you about a recurring experience I had for nearly two years, over encounters with a number of serving officers. I started off just meeting officers, talking to them about my work and their work, and just getting to know them in an informal way. I travel a lot for work, and at some point in a conversation, I'd mention a place I was headed to, or somewhere else I would soon be traveling. Literally every initial encounter I had with a police officer would end in an eerily similar way. A business card, or an offer of a phone number of a friend, or an email of another person whom I could contact in this place or that, would be handed over to me *"just in case."* "Just in case of what?" would be the thought backing up my spoken and genuine words of thanks to this officer. But the answer was clear — just in case I was ever in a jam, just in case I needed help, and needed someone to call on. The motivation for these sincerely moving overtures of caretaking from multiple individuals from multiple police forces was staggering. There is danger everywhere. The overarching world view. The world is terribly dangerous. AND…. the only thing you can trust is a personal contact. There is no system that is trustworthy. There is no force that protects us. There is nothing we can count on other than small sets of individuals. And officer after officer extended this care to me, a stranger, nobody special. They want to protect. They want to save. But the world is a big place. And individuals can only do so much. This stays with me, an experience simultaneously beautiful, touching, and terribly, terribly sad.

This experience, consistently reinforced, led me to think about the error in how we understand the idea of serving and protecting. It seems that in both directions this conjures simultaneous images of servants and warlords, an almost oxymoronic definition of the role of police. Clearly that is deeply problematic, both for the public and for the law enforcement officers.

Jack has a few training points that he continually reinforces. One of these is that whenever role (i.e. the role law enforcement officials are expected to reveal as professionals) and voice conflict, then people, the public, will only believe the voice. When you're serving as a law enforcement official, you are expected to play a very specific role. If your voice (or your posture or your nonverbal communication) says something that conflicts with the role you ought to be revealing as a professional, the person will believe the voice rather than the role. Implicit in this training point, and in the need to reiterate it ad infinitum, is that there is a disconnect between what law enforcement officials often *think* they are communicating, and what their voice and body and manner actually do communicate to the public. What then *is* the role of the police? It seems a new conception of this is long overdue.

As I sat with these new experiences and information I began to wonder what would happen if we could shift our understanding, and try a new metaphor. Perhaps we could instead look at our own bodies and think of our skin. Think about skin for a moment: *It* serves and it protects. My skin polices my body. It takes care of me. It feels for me. It keeps me protected. It lets some things in and keeps other things out. It is a *part* of me. How might our relationship to policing change if this were the metaphor through which we understood their "force"?

The starting assumption that often pervades sensitivity and communication trainings is that people would act differently if only they could see things from another person's point of view. A concept that arose during our project was the realization of this as an impossibility. It implies that you can take off your perspective and slip into someone else's. But that's impossible. You can't remove yourself from a situation. You can never see through someone else's eyes. That would be like asking yourself to remove your own skin and to put on someone else's, as a kind of suit.

What we found was that in addition to being impossible, putting focus on this goal was not liberating but rather distracting from another, related, yet substantively different opportunity that promotes the general idea of "emotional competence." Instead of focusing on trying to be someone else, we can try to increase our own awareness of the different components of our own perspective, and our ability to manage these components in crisis. The only thing you can do is to understand all the different things that go into making up *your* perception of a situation, and to try to perceive the things that may be going on from another person's perspective simultaneously.

We have to train ourselves to listen with all of our senses. We can do that. If we give it a little bit of time. And a lot of validation. The aim of the final six-week project became to begin to *find a path to shifting patterns of thinking* in intense, crisis oriented situations. Our challenge at the final stage of our collaboration was the question: How can we move our manner of thinking and acting from a place of rigidity to a place of fluidity?

Untitled

A serving officer

I am human.
I have feelings.
I cry but I don't show you.
I love with all my heart.
I will die to save you.
I protect you.
I don't sleep.

I see what you can not see.

I am a target.

I am a friend, a husband, a brother, an
uncle. I can listen I can judge I can kill.
But you see me as an oppressor
an occupying army.
You see me as evil. You will never understand,
but I understand you.

We are both human.

ℭ ||| ℬ

Our Approach: Active Listening and Experiential Learning

The Hostage Negotiation Team's motto is *"Talk to me."* Jack spends the majority of his training time working with people on learning active listening skills. He has an arsenal of funny videos to lure you into his sobering case studies of how a lack of active listening can result in tragic miscarriages of justice. Active listening is no joke.

How do we design a class that requires active listening in the learners? We model it. Here are a few of the principles we employed in designing the experiential learning sessions:

1. *This is a project, not a class. It is something we are making together. The content and material of the class is you.*
2. *There is a journey we will steer you through, but most of the details of this are openings, rather than conclusions an authority is driving you toward.*
3. *We will simulate, to a small degree, the quality of uncertainty that characterizes the negotiation of emergent crisis situations:*

    You will be asked to do things you are not expert in.

    You will be paired with people very different from you.

    You will travel to areas of town you are not familiar with.

    You will be asked to do tasks that do not let you attach to a concrete or specific role.

You will be asked to do more than is humanly possible in an incredibly short period of time.

These principles were derived from the intersection of Jack's experience training Hostage Negotiators and Rachel's approach to creating collaborative theater. A mutual goal in our work is to achieve individual and group active listening, and to have everyone working toward a common goal that they perceive is more important than any individual stakeholder's goals. You check your ego at the door and you open yourself to listen to a situation with all of your senses. Engaging the senses was our key to starting on this final section of collaboration.

As mentioned above, the bedrock of Jack's training for hostage negotiators is active listening. In the following section, he outlines the core ideas he conveys to his colleagues and those entering his field.

Jack: Core Concepts of Hostage Negotiation

The most basic tools in a negotiator's toolbox are active listening communication skills and empathy. Active listening is a way of listening and responding to another person that improves mutual understanding. These skills help to lower emotions and start the process of developing rapport. Often when people talk to each other, they do not listen attentively. They are easily distracted, half listening, half (usually) thinking about something else.

The negotiator must give specialized attention to matters of importance. If an issue is important to the individual the negotiator is negotiating with, then the negotiator should consider that issue to be important, whether or not it is important to the negotiator.

The negotiator must possess the human qualities of compassion and common sense; these two critical traits, along with empathy, will greatly assist in managing high emotion. Negotiators must have the ability to remain calm under emotionally demanding circumstances.

Demonstrating self-control is one of their most important attributes. The negotiator is expected to possess the ability to set his or her emotions aside during tense negotiations, be non-judgmental in their approach, and to do so, in most instances, in a harmonious fashion. They are required to bring a lifetime of experience to the table in order to manage potentially volatile situations, and be the calming voice of reason in the most unreasonable and chaotic of situations. Being a negotiator mandates being a mature and stable individual who can adapt to quickly changing circumstances. They do this in highly unpredictable situations, knowing that the stakes are high, understanding that if they fail in their negotiation attempt, lives could very well be lost.

Hostage negotiators generally utilize the behavioral change stairway model (Vecchi et al 2005) developed by the Federal Bureau of Investigation (FBI). The model has five steps that are to be completed in succession for a behavioral change to take place. For example, a negotiator must successfully listen (Step 1) before he or she can express empathy (Step 2). See the chart below for the five stages or steps. Likened to climbing stairs in a house, if you try to bypass a step or two to save time, it can be done, but it will take much more effort to get to the top destination.

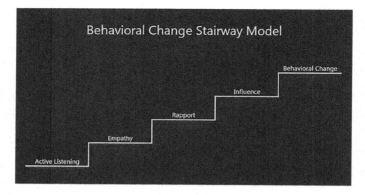

A brief description of the five steps follows:

1. *Active Listening:* This first step establishes the foundation for the ensuing steps, and involves techniques aimed at establishing a relationship between the negotiator and person in crisis. Active Listening encourages conversation through the use of open ended questions, paraphrasing their understanding of the individual message, and attempts to identify and confirm emotions expressed by the individual, and it utilizes intentional pauses in the conversation for emphatic effect.

2. *Empathy:* The second step is to convey empathy to the individual in crisis. Empathy suggests the negotiator has an understanding of the perceptions and feelings of the other side. It is not the same as sympathy, which is to feel sorry for someone's misfortune, and it does not mean that you necessarily agree with the individual. This is an important element in furthering the relationship between the negotiator and individual and can be accomplished through a tone of voice that is genuine and conveys interest and concern. The negotiator's tone of voice indicates his or her attitude; this speaks louder than words. A calm, controlled demeanor may be more effective than a

brilliant argument. A common negotiator mistake when trying to use empathy wisely is the statement "I know exactly how you feel!" The fact is that we could never really know how someone is exactly feeling.

A personal note: I once said exactly this to a man standing on the Verrazano Narrows Bridge that links Brooklyn to Staten Island. The man standing on the girder of the bridge retorted that I don't know exactly how he feels, because if I did, I would be standing right next to him wanting to jump! This man had no family, no friends, no job and no money; I had all of these, so how could I possibly know exactly how he feels; I can't! I apologized to the man for my insensitive comment, which he accepted and started the process of developing rapport between us, where he ultimately came down off his perch and onto the roadway. I have since modified my approach after that powerful life-lesson encounter to say "I can only imagine how you might be feeling; can you tell me about it?"

3. *Rapport:* The third step is established through the negotiator's active listening and expression of empathy, which will lead to increased trust between the parties. The negotiator continues to build rapport through conversation that focuses on face saving for the other side, positive reframing of the situation, and exploring areas of common ground.

4. *Influence:* Once rapport has been firmly established, the negotiator is in a position to begin to make suggestions to the other side, to explore potential and realistic options to the conflict, and to consider the likely alternatives available to the individual.

5. *Behavioral Change:* The final step is dependent upon how thoroughly and prudently the negotiator passed through the first four steps. If the negotiator has established a solid relationship with the individual in crisis, then he or she will be able

> to propose solutions to the conflict that will, hopefully, effect the desired behavioral change.
>
> It is important not to try to skip any of the steps. As indicated, you can do this — but the overall effort will be that much greater. When negotiators push too hard for a "quick resolve", then the other side will push back equally as hard, by saying NO, I'm not ready yet! — or by doing something worse.

The project Jack and I were developing arrived at the all-inclusive title, *Emotional Competence in Policing Project.* However, emotions are a bit of a red herring to build a training upon, as they don't help build reliable technique. They are subjective, fleeting and very difficult to standardize. In theater and other performance training, you learn that trying to create or to perform an emotion itself is a dead end. There are many different pathways into generating the *opportunity* for an emotion to arise, either in the audience or in the performers. However, emotion itself is a useless tool in the staging of a play, because it is an unpredictable by-product of a character's identifiable situated actions. If, by contrast, we can identify the given circumstances of a character, then we can identify or even manipulate where someone's actions can lead to a particular outcome.

We don't need to apply psychological labels to our experiences when we could just pay attention to the impact of the given circumstances on a person, or a group of people in an environment. Because we actually sense things, because we have the input from all of our senses coming in and affecting our beings, we don't need to think about how we emote in a situation. Instead we can concentrate on the input that's registering. That becomes a more practical, level playing field. We can see what in our environment affects us bodily, and then move our awareness of our perceptions further in and then further out, to help tune ourselves into understanding what we're working with in any interpersonal situation.

Jack and I found our "in" to the experiential learning sessions to be focusing on different ways of tuning-in. Our first three sessions focused on the individual, guiding participants toward a greater understanding of their own perceptions, and of how these inform their behavior and perspectives. The final three sessions steered the group toward looking at interpersonal awareness, their perspectives in a social setting, and called on participants to apply their tools of awareness to different contexts. We arrived at a point in the fifth session in which the students themselves declared that the only way to navigate these paths was through compassion — a word we had not yet mentioned. Yet this was where we were intending to arrive. The last session focused on compassion in crisis.

Active Listening Always

Teniece Divya Johnson

Active listening always
Impacts the quality of our relationships
Listening is a skill that takes much practice
Much like a gymnast practicing back flips
Or any sport to become the first round draft pick

Active Listening always builds trust
No defensive backlash, only truth and just (ice)
This will help Get –to- the- point
No need to go around in circles that cause confusion
We need those revolutions to find
solutions

Your eyes may tell you one thing
Your ears will share another
Your instinct whispers truth
Patience, Practice and
Wisdom reveal what lies undercover

Freedom beats fear
Release the ego that may cloud causing confusing
Your vulnerability allows
the vibrations to flow unobstructed
– all energies connected
When you give 100% attention

Your eyes may tell you one thing
Your ears will share another
Your instinct whispers truth
Patience, Practice and
Wisdom reveal what lies undercover

Imagining a situation
Where all parties at the end
Are better off and giving thanks
Now that's a win win

ভ IV ৵

Formal Learning Objectives

While the main portion of the course was one in which participants co-created their learning environment, we did set out formal learning objectives and goals for each session. The formal learning objectives included:

1. To bolster participants' ability to adapt their behavior in different and difficult circumstances

2. To enhance participants' experience with empathy and creative thinking

3. To engage "personality plasticity" and to help participants understand you're not being duplicitous when you change and adapt your behavior according to the environment

4. To activate self-compassion, to reflexively understand your position within the realities of working in the job you have.

The session by session goals were outlined as follows:

1. Developing an awareness of your surroundings and stimuli from the external environment, with particular attention to the senses

2. Developing an awareness of how one's own background, thoughts, and context can influence the surrounding environment

3. Utilizing case studies and policing scenarios, to increase officers' level of awareness of how the environment and the individual's context can contribute to a successful or destructive negotiation

4. Developing and analyzing new experiences of empathy when looking at a situation from the outside
   Performance poets included as collaborators

5. Developing and analyzing new experiences of empathy when experiencing a situation from the inside
   Performance poets included as collaborators

6. Using compassion and self-compassion in crisis situations
   Presenting parallel case studies and principles from the fields of Emergency Medicine and the NYPD's Hostage Negotiation Team

See Something Say Something

Maurice Emerson Decaul

The Cop said to the old guy, "You piece of
shit, get the fuck off this
train." Then

the Cop said to him, "You piece of shit get
the fuck out this
station." Afterwards

the Cop turned around, seemingly
needing from the rest of us some affirmation
shook his head & then he shook his head.

$$\text{CR} \ \vee \ \text{RQ}$$

The Curriculum

Session 1: You are here

The first day of the experiential learning sessions was upon us. I would be meeting the group for the first time, and I would be working with Chris Honeyman and Maria Volpe in the classroom. Some of the participants would be students, some would be police officers, others would be conflict management professionals. At the start of the class I wanted to circumvent any role identification (so that people wouldn't segregate themselves into cliques based on job or status) and to establish co-ownership of the process. I made a few choices to facilitate this. I left introductions until the end of class, I put the group into randomized subgroups in which they had to do time-limited activities that required sharing personal information, and I also offered lunch every day for the cohort, as a way of making this more of a project than a class: "it's a place where we share activities together." The theme of this class was *You are here,* and the design of this class was intended to express the sense that they had entered into something that had already begun. They had entered into their lives.

Key day one activities:

1. Draw a mental map of how you got here today.

a. Include one sound you heard and a description of one thing you touched.

b. Make a list of everywhere in New York City and the surrounding counties where you've travelled this week.

2. Take those maps and lists to your small group. Each group has a map of the tri-state area.

a. With markers, map your usual routes on the group map

b. Identify two areas you *don't* go to — one you're curious about, but don't have a reason to go to, and one you feel like you don't belong in. Write those down — we'll collect them, and use them to set your homework assignment.

3. Foreground, middle ground, background
a. in small groups, consider an image. Describe it.
b. now focus just on the background
c. now focus just on the middle ground
d. now focus just on the foreground

How do you now describe the image differently?

4. Listen to the room.
a. In a circle, sit with your eyes closed. We're going to listen to the room for one minute.

b. Now try to focus in on any sounds you hear outside of the room — the background sounds, the far-away sounds. Call out anything you hear.

c. Now focus in on the sounds in the middle distance — inside the room, perhaps in the hallway, until maybe a few feet in front of your face.

d. Now focus in on those sounds closest to you.

5. Field observation.
a. Get into pairs.

b. Your partner picks a location for you in the building [the building was large, with many kinds of spaces.]. You will both travel there.
c. Your partner will ask you to close your eyes, and then give you a series of prompts to describe, one at a time, for one full minute each:
> what you *hear*
> what you *smell*
> what you *taste*
> what you *feel*
> and then to open your eyes, and describe what you *see*.

Your partner will document your observations. Then you will switch and repeat the task.

6.   Gather together as one group again.
The pairs will share their findings from the observation exercise. We will share the group maps and discuss patterns of movement and what we overlook in our daily movement patterns. We will now introduce ourselves by name, and share the places we don't go to.

You will be given a specific location to travel to, based on where you identified you *don't* go to. During the next week you will travel there to repeat the Field Observation project by yourself, following an observation log we will hand out.

7.   Discussion about this project.
This is the Emotional Competence in Policing Project. Let's focus on the word *project*. In light of what you've done today and what you see you'll be doing going forward, what does that mean to you?

The discussion following this set-up leads us to identifying this as a learning environment that we are co-creating. We will be building it together.

A Place of Peace

Jenny Pacanowski

I don't usually look for places
Maybe people
Maybe noticing drug addicts
Maybe drunks
Maybe disorderly types
Maybe just guns
Weapons to analyze
That smell
Always present
Gunpowder
I can still smell
The unfiltered air
Sticks to my nose hairs
Seeps into the crevasses of my nasal cavity
Ballistics
I am Ballistics
Splatter
Shooter
The ear plugs have molded to my physique
The pleasant shape of my skull
Distorted by their presence
Protective presence

My direction is clear
I peel the protective layer off my body
The transition is smooth
From the conformity of the uniform

The subway has the usual bumps
Screeches of metal on metal
On my time

I am searching
Searching for a place
Outside my normal view

I look up
Just in time
To slide off my seat
And sail through the doors
Towards the gate

"Crack head theater" is in full swing
They are presenting
A little poetry
A little devastation
A little desperation
The stage in their mind
Ever changing
Just shifting from the crack
To the begging
To the shelter
To the crack
To the next high
To the moment of slight content
To the scheming
To the begging
To the next high

I can hear the birds singing
Not the pigeons
Many varieties
In pitch
In strength of projection
The rustle of the leaves above
Holding the bird's song

My feet move from the concrete
To the gravel crunching

Poking up into the soles of my shoes
I see the grass
Peeking up around the sides
Of this walk

I am staying on course
No time for barefoot in the grass
No time for the massage of
Mother Nature
On the toes of my inner child

I find it
The bench
Worn and brown
Wooden and solid
As I descend into the smell of freshness
The lake breeze is my therapy
I absorb the serenity
Breaking free of the stuffy
The mission complete
Finding a moment of peace
In my mind

Session 2: Wherever you go, you are there

What's the point of all this listening? I had asked the cohort to do pretty far-out exercises without much explanation. In the second session, I needed to address concretely the purpose of these multi-sensory listening exercises. I wanted to do so without changing the tone of the project toward something didactic.

Jack and I facilitated this session together, modeling conversation, reflection and collaboration throughout. Jack has a charming and disarming presence, backed up by a work record that engenders respect and honor. His presence in a room is one of strength and experience. My "character" for this project is to be utterly non-threatening, a warm and kind outsider who is interested and creative, who can unlock places of self-reflection that would normally be guarded. My presence in a room tells the cohort that they're in caring hands, and that I'm taking them somewhere good, even if they have no idea where that will be. Jack and I are a pretty interesting duo. We model similar leadership styles from very different backgrounds. This modeling was the foundation of the session in which a person's *presence* was the core topic. After asking the cohort to tune into their awareness, we would ask them to take one further step, to reflect on just what they as individuals bring into any situation. The message of this class was, "**Wherever you go, you are there.**"

Key day two activities:

1. A ten-minute written reflection on their homework assignment. Include in this time a sketch of the place you went to.

2. Rachel and Jack in discussion, with Rachel basically interviewing Jack. Key questions included:
   What's one thing you wish people would be trained for more?

What are the five top skills you need to have as a hostage negotiator?

Where in life and on the job do you learn these skills?

What's one word you would use to describe every situation you go into as an HN?

3. Group discussion:

How much set-up did we do last week? *Not much.*

How much context did I give you for why you were doing certain things? *Not much.*

Shall we talk about that a bit, and what you guys experienced in your field assignment?

Wait, before we do that, I have another question for you, Jack: How much set-up and context do you have when you go into work every day, for what is going to happen? *Not much.*

The way we're organizing this project is so that the sessions and the activities model some of the key lessons that are vital to Emotional Competence in Policing.

We're going to ask you to do things, to get into situations, and to let any learning come from them.

This characteristic of uncertainty in the activities should also make it apparent how important time for reflection and discussion are.

4. I'd like you to take the reflections you wrote, and give us the highlights. You're going to tell us your name, your place you went to, you'll show us your sketch, and then you'll read your written reflection.

5. Group discussion: On competence

This is called the Emotional Competence in Policing Project. This week I want to speak about the word Competence. What does that mean?

To be able to do something.

To have the skills and to know how to use them.

What does tuning in to our senses have to do with that?

Our senses, our ability to perceive and to be aware of what it is we are perceiving, is the first step in building up a facility, a competence, with our emotions. We have to be able to recognize what we're feeling and what others are feeling in order to be able to have a real competence with managing these things. We have tools. We just don't take time to learn how to use them.

There are a couple ideas we'll work with over the course of this project. Last week was *you are here,* and tuning your senses. This week, we'll add to that and say, *wherever you go, you are there.*

That's pretty big, right? Let's talk about that.

You can't separate work and life. You can't remove your self from any situation you are in. And if you think you can, you're fooling yourself. And when you fool yourself, you miss sometimes vital information, about yourself or about someone else or about a situation. And this can lead to big mistakes.

6.   Group discussion: On role identification
Jack, can you tell a couple stories now from your work where you've seen people try to take themselves out of the equation? And what I mean by that in this case really is, when you've seen people you work with act like their role as an officer, rather than the person you know them to be?

This type of over-identification with a role happens throughout all walks of life of course, with a dad/mom saying "cause I'm the dad/mom, that's why", rather than listening to what their child needs or really being aware of what they themselves are feeling. The first step in to being able to step back from this type of over-identification with a role is awareness — awareness of what you're sensing, and an ability to perceive those sensations without letting them control your actions.

7.　Practical application of these ideas: Wherever you go, you are there. Let's practice with some of this.

Activity:

a. Draw a floor plan of a place where you feel really comfortable. Try to be as specific as possible about the details.
b. Write a number from zero to your age on the page. Write one memory (of any type) next to each number.
c. Share with a partner, building a picture of the floor plan and then listing the numbers and the memories.

Discussion:

Wherever you go, you are there. You carry all of these memories, places and experiences around with you as well, everywhere you go. You carry your spaces of care and comfort. You also carry your memories in all types of sensory packaging.

8.　Fieldwork assignment for next week: You're going to do another observation in your location this week. But this week, you're going to put *yourself* there.

Activity:

Travel to your assigned location.

Walk around the entire perimeter of the area. OBSERVE what you perceive through all your senses. Use SOFT FOCUS.

Once you've walked the perimeter, stop and answer the following questions:

> *Describe everything you hear, right now.*
> *Describe everything you taste, right now.*
> *Describe everything you smell, right now.*
> *Describe everything you feel, right now.*
> *Describe everything you see, right now*

Now, choose one specific location to station yourself. This can be the same place as last week, or it could be a new one if you'd prefer to change. You will need to be comfortable here for approximately the next hour.

You will now observe the changing environment, and connect these to memories from your life.

You will focus on one sense at a time, for a period of 10 minutes each.

You will take a note of what you observe through that sense, recording at least 5 notes for each sense.

Remember to observe across locations: foreground, middle-ground and background.

Once you take note of an observation, then let your mind wander. Write a reflection on what this observation reminds you of? What memories from your life does this observation connect to?

Don't judge, go with your gut. Approach this process of connection through soft focus.

Session 3: Wherever you are, you belong

Finding ways of navigating your sensory input in a Policing context

The biggest underlying issue at this point became "Belonging." It's all well and good to tune into your senses and to become more aware of who you are, but what if you're not in your private space? What if you're on the job? What if you're acting as "police" and not yourself? The message we needed to reinforce for the cohort at this time was precisely the error in this thinking. No matter what role you're taking on, **wherever you go, you belong**.

At the top of this session, we discussed what a police officer's job is. Zeroing in on the slogan "to serve and protect", we started to unpack what that meant. Through discussion, we looked at this from different angles, and tried on a few ways of understanding it that are different than the ones we normally think about. Building on the work from the previous "tuning in" sessions, we hit upon the metaphor of the skin. Our skin as a sensory organ, which shields us, and protects us, which regulates our different bodily systems, but which undeniably belongs to our bodies, seemed a revelatory comparison.

Jack then turned the discussion toward a direct policing context. He wove a journey through personal and public examples of police, both in successfully using active total sensory listening, and in historical and contemporary examples of missed opportunities that result in tragically mishandled crises. The main learning points did not directly deal with the examples he enumerated, but rather centered around ways of entering into a process of active listening. These he describes below, to introduce an audience who have never engaged with these concepts before to ways of starting out with the practice of active listening. For those with more experience with this style of communication, these summaries are worth reflecting upon as a way of articulating technique.

Jack: On Active Listening

Emotion Labeling: It is important for the emotions of the person speaking to be acknowledged. Identifying the person's emotions validates what they are feeling instead of minimizing it. During a negotiation, people can act with their emotions and not from a more cognitive perspective. Labeling and acknowledging their emotions helps restore the balance. It's OK if you get the emotion wrong, for example, if the negotiator says "you seem sad." The other side may retort by saying "I'm not sad, I'm angry!" The negotiator would then apologize for the misinterpretation, but will now have the emotion identified and can start the process of building rapport.

Paraphrasing: This includes repeating what the person said in a much shorter format that is in your own words, while also making sure to not minimize what the person has experienced.

Reflecting/Mirroring: When the person has finished speaking, reflecting and mirroring is a much shorter option compared to paraphrasing as it includes repeating the last words the person said. If the person concluded by saying, "…and this really made me angry," you would say, "It really made you angry."

Reflecting/Mirroring should be limited to strictly repeating no more than 3 or 4 of the last words spoken by a person. It might seem silly or even odd to do this, but try it — you will see it helps validate with the speaker that you are listening and understanding.

Effective Pauses/Silence: Research has shown a major difference between expert hostage and crisis negotiators and non-experts is that experts listen much more than they speak. A general rule for the hostage negotiator is 80 percent listening and 20 percent talking. Part of listening includes utilizing silence, and pausing before taking your turn to speak. Also described as dynamic inactivity, silence allows the other person to continue speaking, while combining it with pausing prior to speaking helps calm a situation. Again, remember, calming the situation is critical as it helps move the person from acting out of their emotions to a mindset that is more cognitive based. Whenever emotional levels are up, rational thinking is down; it is when rational thinking is down when we make wrong decisions.

"I" Messages: This is used to counteract statements made by the person that are not conducive towards working collaboratively. The active listener states, "I feel___ when you ___ because ___." The 'I – When – Because' equation provides a "timeout" or reality check to the other person, letting them know you are trying to work together and they, from your perspective, are not. It is important to be mindful when using this to not do it in a way (be aware of your tone) that is aggressive and creates an impression of being judgmental.

Open-ended Questions: Asking open-ended questions invites the person to speak longer. Thus it can help diffuse the tension as well as provide you valuable information and insight into their perspective of the situation. Open-ended questions discourage a simple yes or no response. Whenever utilizing open-ended questions, always lead with 'how, what, where, who, and when.' This will convey sincerity and interest in understanding the other side, and fosters continued dialog.

Minimal Encouragers: What seem like simple verbal actions, such as "mmm," "okay," uh huh, and "I see," and nonverbal gestures like head nodding, further establish the building of rapport with the person, by you subtly inviting the person to continue speaking.

Summarizing: Summarizing is an extended version of paraphrasing. It is wrapping up everything the person said, including the elements important to the person as well as acknowledging the person's emotions. Summarizing validates for the person that they have been heard and understood. This is critical to do, as it can bring a sense of relief to the person and reduce their actions being dictated by their emotions.

Summarizing is also a valuable tool for a negotiator to use when he or she is unsure what to do or say next. Summarizing what the person has said has multiple benefits in this situation. First, it buys you time, and as already stated, slowing the process down is an important element to contribute to a peaceful resolution.

Second, summarizing can further contribute to the negotiator building rapport and developing trust. Rapport and trust then allow the negotiator to eventually move towards influencing the person to reappraise their situation, and consider alternatives — suggestions from the negotiator, and eventually, a resolution.

After Jack's presentation, the cohort was then tasked with a three-part fieldwork assignment activating the learning points from this session. It built upon the previous weeks' work combining active listening, reflections on the job of a police officer, and this week's intentional interpersonal engagement.

Part One:
Travel to your assigned location.

Walk around the perimeter of the area, with soft focus and with awareness.

Once you've walked the perimeter, stop and consider the following questions:

What protects this place?
What regulates this place?
What are the sensations of this place?

Answer these questions by collecting information that you can bring back and share in small groups next week. You will collect the following:

    One rhythm
    One sound
    One smell
    Three images
    Two tactile sensations
    One taste
    Three memories from your three times visiting
    this location

You can bring in objects, photographs, drawings, voice recordings, words, and anything else you can think of to complete this assignment.

Part Two:

Approach an individual on site. Ask them if they will help you with a project you're doing. You can describe the project to them. You will be asking them to simply answer a series of questions. Ask them if you can record their answers using your phone. (Don't worry if they say no, you can offer instead to just write down their responses.) The questions you can ask them are:

    Describe to me everything you hear, right now.
    Describe to me everything you taste, right now.
    Describe to me everything you smell, right now.
    Describe to me everything you feel, right now.
    Describe to me everything you see, right now.

Thank them.
    Ask them if you can take their photograph as well. (Once again, it's fine if they say no.)

Part Three:

Bring in an additional object for next week that is meaningful to you.

Lament For Officer Friendly

Maurice Emerson Decaul

I heard a woman lamenting the death of
Officer Friendly
he was a pillar in her community. Once
when she & her friends
were about to get into trouble, it was
Officer Friendly
who knowing their parents, took them
home. Officer Friendly
was also the crossing guard. Officer
Friendly would sometimes show up
in the cafeteria of her elementary school.
He always carried
a smile to share with her & the other
children. Her own cousin
had been an Officer Friendly. He was
struck & killed on a highway
outside Chicago, a week before leaving
the force because
he'd become disillusioned. She was
terribly angry at the death
of Officer Friendly because in his wake
came a new Officer
who was less than friendly, who patrolled
the neighborhood
but knew no one, who rarely carried a
smile or shared a laugh
who over her fifty years had developed
into an adversary.

Session 4: Crossing contexts and reading a static scene

At this point in the process we began transitioning to expand our introspection to include the public sphere. What happens when we incorporate others into our practice of awareness? As a practical "provocation", during this session five poets from Poetic Theater joined our cohort. Jenny, Allison, Maurice, Kelly and Teniece were now a part of the group, and they were integrated without much explanation. The group work now included "outsiders" — who were treated as if they had been there all along.

These weren't just any random people, however; they were artists. They are people who have made radically alternative life choices, and they were a group that came from very different walks of life. Also as artists, they have been trained in the practice of observation, reflection, and listening. They are also five people who are exceptionally interested in the world around them. Incorporating them into the activities opened a new dimension for the participants. Likewise, this was a revelatory experience for the artists. They had a basic idea of what they were getting into, and they had been given task 3 from the previous week's field assignment; but much as with the rest of the participants, they were to learn by doing as they went along.

This session was broken up into two distinct parts. The first was about *crossing contexts,* identifying emotions, and experiencing someone else attempting to put themselves in your shoes. Key points of consideration for this are, what is happening when someone else tries to understand you? The second part flipped this investigation and put participants in the role of someone making sense of a situation external to them. The activity animating this investigation focused on *reading a static scene,* with the key question here being: What happens when you try to understand someone else?

Part one:

1. Get into small groups of four. Folks who were here last week will present their fieldwork experience of their place to these small groups.

2. Still in your small groups, make a list of all the emotions you can think of. Share the master list with the group.

3. Individually, take out your personal object, and write three words that you relate to that object.

4. Unpack each word, one at a time, in a short descriptive free write.

5. Get in pairs and swap writing. Your partner will read aloud your words describing the object, without any context, just your words. How do your words sound different, coming from someone else's mouth? How does it feel to hear your words? How does hearing them from someone else make you understand your own feelings and emotions differently?

Part two:

This part of the session asked small groups to read a scene through an analysis of the "given circumstances," a technique from theatre in the Stanislavsky tradition that breaks down the different parts of a situation into specific contexts that will allow an actor to play the situation. The fundamental question for the participants here is: How do you apply the information from your sensory input and your own personal perspective, and make meaning out of something that is external to you? Can you ever actually put yourself in someone else's shoes (remembering Jack's question to the man on the bridge and his response to "I know exactly how you feel")? What transformations happen when you *try* to put yourself into someone else's shoes?

Activity:

Look at this photo and describe as much as you can about it, according to the observable given circumstances. You can read *any* scene following these categories.

The World — (when/historical, where/geographical, political, social, etc. — everything about the environment)

Time (character's relationship to immediacy, time pressure, etc.)

Character (who is in the picture?)

Relationships (what is the relationship between the characters?)

Events (what is happening?)

Wants (what do the characters want?)

Tactics (how are they going about trying to get what they want?)

Discussion:

The groups then shared their analysis of the photo with the whole cohort. What happened in the second part of the session is that each group made assumptions about the image based largely on the dress and their awareness of the social and political landscape of the time period. What was a bunch of kids at a puppet show, became terrified or angry children in turmoil in World War II. Each of the groups had particular assumptions about the context of the time period, and made broad generalizations about what life was like for everyone who wore a certain set of clothes. They were shocked both to hear the similarities between the groups' stories, and to see the underlying prejudice that came out of a place of interest, care and empathy.

Activity:

Now we're going to read a real life scene.

As a small group, you're going to go out and find a location with people within a five-minute walk from here. Make sure it is a place you have never simply stopped to observe before. Make sure it is a very specific location.

You're going to observe it for 60 seconds and record the given circumstances. Then you will come back and describe the location as a group.

Homework:

After the groups came back and described their location, they were given a task to do independently in preparation for the next week's session: You will then individually come up with challenges for people in your group to undertake next week. Something achievable, something visible, an action. We'll use these next week.

The Ideal Police Academy, Part One

Jenny Pacanowski

Low lights illuminate the stage. It is a classroom with a whiteboard and some desks and chairs pushed against the walls. There is movement on the floor of the stage but it is difficult to make out the shapes…of the beings…

A tall broad shouldered man named Gary enters with 4 new recruits.

2 men

Caleb and Dave

2 women

Nissa and Jackie

Gary: Well cadets, here is your first "hands on" exercise. Now that you have passed the tests in emotional ompetency…we are going to put your knowledge of patience and compassion TO THE TEST!

(He flips on the lights of the classroom. The stage is now bright and full of puppies of all breeds and sizes, between 2 and 6 months old.)

Jackie: *(proclaims)* What are WE going to do with a bunch of dogs???

Gary: *(smiles)* Serve and Protect them!!!! Of Course!! With professionalism!

Caleb: But they can't talk!

Gary: Well, that's not entirely true. They have their own language!

(he points his finger in the air)

Now, let's see what skills you really have! Get the puppies to safety.

Each cadet individually tries to scoop up many puppies or one at a time and put them in the playpens and crates. They fumble around and the puppies squirm away, running through legs and jumping out of the playpens. Eventually the cadets are all panting and sweating.

Gary watches laughing to himself

Dave: *(highly frustrated, with one particular puppy, winds up and kicks the pup into the crate and slams the door):* Ha! Got ya now!

(In one swift motion Jackie pins Dave against the wall.)

Jackie: What the hell?

(She shakes him as he squirms)

Gary: Freeze!!!! Everyone!

(Jackie drops Dave to the floor)

Gary: As you have been taught, there are many ways to accomplish a task especially when dealing with other beings. There is a forceful way which can lead to violence, riots, chaos, looting, etc.... This could cause undue harm

to you, your fellow officers and the people you are trying
to protect.

However as a police officer, you want to build respect
through cooperation, awareness and understanding in the community YOU SERVE!

Dave: How are we supposed to learn that by wrangling
puppies?!

Gary: Start by changing perceptions on how to achieve
your task. Your perception is what, Dave?

Dave: To do this efficiently and quickly. Since they can't
talk and they are smaller than me. I assumed it would be
easy to wrangle them to the destination of confinement.

Gary: By using the word, "wrangling" what does that
imply?

Jackie: That you will be using force.

Gary: YES! However by simply using different WORDS
could start a new thought process and action.

And what about the assumptions that because something
is smaller it is easier to move?

Caleb: Assumptions are dangerous. The puppies may be smaller
however their quantity is more than us.

Nissa: What about using the word, "Gather" or "
Corralling."

Gary: Not exactly. How about persuading or even better
MOTIVATING?

And what about the idea of "confinement" being "
safety?"

Jackie: Maybe instead of confine, it could be a safe place f
or observation? Or maybe escort home…?

Gary: Possibly….

*(Gary walks to a jar by the door. It contains bacon strips. He
pulls out six pieces.)*

*(The six puppies notice his movements and start following him.
He moves from the door to find an expandable large exercise
playpen. He opens it up, places himself INSIDE…..and the
puppies follow. He closes the entrance around them. He gives
each puppy a piece of bacon.)*

**Gary: Nissa, give me the marrow bones from the crates.
Dave, give me the tug ropes from the floor. Caleb, grab
some tennis balls from the basket in the corner.**

*(As Gary places each toy in the ex-pen, the puppies happily play
as he REMOVES himself)*

Dave: So, we are supposed to give bones and toys to
criminals to keep an eye on them in one place.

Gary: *(looks at the other cadets): What do you think?*

Jackie: I don't think it was about treats or toys.

Gary: Why?

*Jackie: It was about motivation and how to change our
perception on achieving tasks without force.*

Nissa: (sarcastically) I think we are starting with
the puppies so Dave can kick them and not be sued.

Caleb: Or because they don't speak, so we must work
extra hard about thinking how to communicate. First we
can adapt the way we think and then add words to it. So when we
work with people we can be more effective in
communicating.

Gary: Let's break for lunch!

Session 5: Acting and listening — reading a live action scene

The fifth session was where the dramaturgical climax need-ed to be. They *need* to have a breakthrough. I believed it had begun the previous week with the "given circumstances" activity, and the intention was to ramp that up today, put-ting it into action, and putting themselves in the hot-seat. Poet Kelly Tsai kicked off this hot-seating by facilitating a few activities followed by readings of the writings.

> A guided free write with the prompt: "What you don't know about me."
> A guided free write with the prompt: "My ideal police academy."
> Kelly calls on individuals to read out what they wrote. This was uncomfortable at times because people felt this was very exposing. However, with Kelly's warm and inspiring leadership, several people came forward to read their pieces, and with each reading came an appreciation for their words, their insight and their bravery.

I then got people to write down their specific tasks that they came up with over the preceding week, on small strips of paper which I collected and put in a basket.

They re-formed into small groups, and were tasked with going out to their nearby locations from last week. But this time they would each have a task they would need to do, one at a time. Everyone picked a strip out of the basket — it was luck of the draw what they would be asked to do. These tasks included activities such as: buy a stranger a coffee, help someone cross the street, sing a song to a stranger, etc. The groups would go out and position themselves on location, taking up the place of an observer while one member of their group took a turn completing their task. The observation group would record what they saw happening, following the "given circumstances" breakdown. Then the next member of the group would do their task, and the group would observe and record. Once completed, they were to return to discuss what happened as a whole group.

People returned and then talked about what they found. There was such discrepancy in how individuals saw the same experience. It was staggering. Individuals in the same group described the situations and what they observed, and what they experienced, in completely different ways. They had even read the tone of the situation entirely differently.

The explanation for these differences was clear: *all of the specifics for how people read the situation came from their own previous personal experiences.* If they were conditioned to be hyper-aware of danger, they would read a situation as dangerous. If they had had ample experience with dealing with harmless yet annoying people being flirtatious, they could read a situation as funny rather than threatening. Job experience, social experience, gender, socio-economic class, everything from the cohort's individual backgrounds came into play when doing this group task, and deeply colored their readings of the same scene.

This discussion led into a reflection on how entrenched we are in our own perspective, even when we're trying to be objective. How could we possibly ever come to a common understanding of anything then, the cohort lamented! Will we never be able to stand in someone else's shoes? What can possibly guide us through?

I didn't offer anything but a "Yes. That is the question. Those are the questions of this project. Now, how will you answer?"

I held a silence of about five full minutes, which, if you've ever held a space in silence before, you will know, feels like an eternity.

Then one person said, "Compassion."
"All right, what about Compassion?"
"Compassion may be our way through."

A full group discussion followed on this subject that was thoughtful, personal, probing and searching. We talked around what compassion is for each of us. Much of what was discussed was that compassion was about seeing and understanding that someone else was in need, and also wanting to help them. It's different from empathy, because you don't have to feel what someone else is feeling, you just have to see that they are experiencing things in a certain way that is most likely different from yours. And, if you're in a position to help, that you can.

They had led themselves toward a powerful personal and policing tool.

Most Officers Fall Back On Drinking
In Order To Deal With Stress

Maurice Emerson Decaul

I just focus on how to use police force to
control the situation, forcing someone to
cooperate with me I think about law
enforcement & police & how that's changed
over my fifty years I speak about something
after much inner debate I protect you I don't
sleep I take risks & chances & I hate that you
don't I see what you can't see I ended up on
the floor I always feel like I feel bad about
people I am a target, I am a friend, a
husband, an uncle I can listen I can judge I
can kill I'm not sure — I started thinking
differently, the 1968 democratic convention
in Chicago I look at the bright/other side of
everything & you're afraid to change I
would train & inform officers how to better
deal with stress I want to fix the system
from inside out I feel bad for you & that's
what you don't know I'm the minority I
would accomplish this by using supportive
hobbies: hiking, photography, scuba, yoga,
shooting NOT TACTICAL BUT
RECREATIONAL I think of the park
experience the smell of trees sit & experience
this place running in the park swimming in
the lake cooking out in the park laying
down on a bench I've worked in
communities that distrust police I feel that
police protect me I would make better use of

the time we have I am a person I recently
broke up with my girlfriend I need to go on
a long drive I can turn the music up I am
alone I say things a lot that I don't mean I do
think you're strong I grew up thinking &
being trained to think the policeman was
my friend I'd be there — I thought I don't
want to hurt anyone I don't want to get hurt
either I'm human I bleed I love I will still do
it I will always come running I am in a place
of peace

Session 6: Compassion and self-compassion in crisis situations

The group, having led themselves toward the tool of compassion, would need that concept unpacked from a practical point of view. What is compassion? How does it fit into policing? How do you apply it in crisis? How do you apply it to yourself, as well?

For the final session, Jack led a talk on this subject of compassion in crisis, from the point of view of working in law enforcement and working specifically within the NYPD. Dr. James O'Shea gave a parallel but shorter talk on the same subject for the final session as well, from the point of view of an emergency room physician working at Newark's Beth Israel Hospital. The common ground for these talks revolved around how individuals, working within a flawed system, deal with and manage crisis constructively. How can recognizing this flawed nature help people be more compassionate toward the people you encounter on the job? And equally important, how can this recognition help you be more compassionate to yourself? Jack's and James's reflections follow:

Jack:

Hostage Negotiators are a group of law enforcement officers who attempt to resolve high-crisis situations with their words. They must have the ability to remain calm under emotionally demanding circumstances. Demonstrating self-control is one of their most critical attributes. The negotiator is expected to possess the ability to set his or her emotions aside during intense negotiations, be non-judgmental in approach, and to do so, in most instances, in a harmonious fashion. They are required to bring a lifetime of experience to the table in order to manage potentially volatile situations, and be the calming voice of reason in the most unreasonable and chaotic of situations. Being a negotiator mandates a mature and stable individual who can adapt to quickly changing circumstances. They do this in highly unpredictable situations, knowing that the stakes are high, understanding that if they fail in their negotiation attempt, lives could very well be lost. A critical component of being a hostage negotiator is to possess the virtue of compassion; without it, one could not hope to have any real measure of success.

In this last section, I spoke to the principles that hostage negotiators rely upon to manage highly emotional encounters. Compassion is something that not everyone possesses. If one does have the good fortune to possess it, then it can be advanced further through life's happenstance. This proved to be the case with me very early in my career.

As a young police officer, I was returning from court on the subway. As I got off the train in Brooklyn, the station clerk called over: "Hey Officer, there's a guy who just went under the turnstile, a homeless guy, just went down toward that end of the platform; didn't pay his fare!" Being new to policing, I wasn't exactly sure what to do with such a minor problem; whether to issue a summons or arrest the man. I decided the best way to handle it without undue expenditure of time would be simply to tell the homeless man to get out on the street, because obviously people cannot use the subway without paying. I walked all the way down to the end of a long platform, where I saw the homeless man, disheveled, about 50 years old — although the streets had not been very kind to him, and so he looked much older. I firmly told him "You didn't pay the fare. You have to leave the subway now!" Having issued a firm statement, I anticipated some degree of aggression, but the man merely said, "Okay Officer, I understand, I will leave." The homeless man and I began walking back down to the exit at the other end of the platform. As we were walking I paid attention to a satchel under his arm, being concerned about possible weapons. I asked firmly, "What do you have in the bag?"

The homeless man replied "Oh, in my bag, Officer, it's a manuscript of a play that I wrote." Taken aback and curious, I asked with some cynicism what the play was about. The homeless man replied that the play was entitled Crabs in a Basket. "It's autobiographical," he said, "it's about my life. If you've ever seen a basket full of crabs, you'll notice that they're all trying to get out. When one finally gets almost to the top of that basket to get out, another crab comes from behind and pulls it back down, grabs it back down. It's kind of like my life... every time I try to get out of the hole that I always find myself in, some force always comes along and brings me back down." I found myself being "blown away." As we approached the exit, I stopped the homeless man and said, "Sir, this ride's on me. Have a good day." I told the man that I hoped to see the play on Broadway someday.

At the cost of irritating the station clerk, I felt that I owed the homeless man that free ride, for teaching me an important life lesson: I had approached the homeless man with a preconceived notion, and had learned that just because the man was homeless didn't mean he was ignorant, or dangerous. This homeless man was down on his luck, yet he was a human being, with a sense of himself and of his circumstances, and an ability to explain them with eloquence — if given the opportunity. Common sense and compassion are not something you can learn in the Police Academy; they are virtues that you either have or you don't. Police officers should assign worth whenever and wherever it is deserved. I have never viewed homeless people in the same regard after that encounter. I thank that homeless man wherever he might be in the world for that powerful life lesson very early on in my career! By the way, I have been looking for that play on Broadway ever since, but still haven't found it.

What I believe the students derived from this personal compelling example was that they must strive hard to develop their emotional competency by nurturing such virtues as common sense, empathy, benevolence and compassion so that it becomes intuitive in their daily interactions with people whom they encounter.

James O'Shea, M.D.

Compassion requires one to recognize the pain experienced by a suffering other, and then to feel motivated to alleviate that suffering. In fields where workers are routinely exposed to the suffering of other people, such as regular police work, hostage negotiation and my own field, emergency medicine, it is important to consider how compassion influences such work.

As with all innate tendencies, there is a wide variety of individualized responses to situations that call for compassion. Some naturally feel a great deal of compassion towards people who are suffering and in crisis, and some others feel very little. That's OK. Probably at the extremes there is more potential for maladaptive responses. If you are crippled by the pathos of a suffering human being and overwhelmed by a pressing urge to help them, you will probably be ineffective as a worker in these situations, or quickly find yourself overwhelmed with compassion fatigue. If you feel too little it may be difficult to connect with the people you serve in a way that allows you to build productive relationships with them. The goal is to simply know the importance of compassion and to develop a mindful appreciation of how you feel compassion as an individual, and how that varies from day to day, and from situation to situation. This skill of self-awareness has been carefully cultivated in the rest of the course and is directly applicable here.

Compassion can be demanding. Anyone can feel moved to help people who are "like them", and there is neuroscience research to show that our compassion responses are loaded with social and racial biases. It is harder to feel compassion for someone in a situation that is considered to be of their own making, or people who may have hurt themselves and other people, and who are living lives that are bizarre and unfathomable to us, and outside our own life experiences. However, we should prepare to be able to do that, because we don't choose whom we are called upon to serve, and if we don't do this emotional work, we will be eaten alive by the job. In human services work there is a documented higher risk of occupational burnout.

Here we discussed Maslach's 3-part definition (Maslach, C. et al 1996, 2016) of burnout, including emotional exhaustion, low sense of personal accomplishment and depersonalization. If you work in a job where you have to deal with other human beings and serve them in some way, you can reasonably expect to have to deal with an element of compassion fatigue, which is related to emotional exhaustion. So, we discussed the implications of that. If you arrive to work in the morning and are fresh, emotionally balanced and ready to serve the good citizens of NYC (or in my case the injured and sick of Newark, New Jersey), then you can think of that as having a pocket full of currency, you're starting the day a rich man or woman. As you encounter other human beings in your work, demands are placed on your energy and your compassion, but it's all good, you can put your hand in your pocket and "spend" some of yourself, and move on. The difficulty is when you put your hand in your pocket and you come up empty, because you haven't been conscious of the need to refill that bank of energy.

But you still have to do the job, right? It's not like you can say to your Sergeant or Medical Director, 'sorry man, I'm all out of caring for today, see you tomorrow'. So you have to take that energy in a sense from your own flesh, the substance of yourself, and it costs more and leaves you more depleted. Being more depleted, you need to close an even bigger energy gap in order to perform the next time, and so you start to circle the toilet. Now if you play that forward, that toilet flush should flush you right out of the job, and maybe you'd end up doing something completely different. But actually, for many people that doesn't happen, either from the constraints of finances or imagination. They just sort of circle the drain emotionally and energetically over a long time, and they develop a new status quo. In an effort to recharge, you might seek support from colleagues who are just as burnt out as you, or seek support in the culture of your profession or organization, which is often simply an institutionalized version of a collection of people across time who were just as burnt out as you.

It doesn't have to be that way, and the greatest weapon against burn-out is self-awareness. When you are in crisis situations where compassion would naturally be called for, and you feel nothing, take that as information for how you are doing. Perhaps you need to make a few regular deposits in that bank of energy that keeps you happy, productive and human.

After a question and answer session with both Jack and James, I asked the participants to reflect on the time we spent together. As a closing exercise, they were asked to generate a set of practical guidelines that they had learned throughout our time together. This is their learning, and their advice to anyone interested in Emotional Competence in complex situations.

Seven Commandments of Emotional Competence

Know yourself.

Observe your surroundings and do not have tunnel vision.

Understand your current state of mind and your past.

Listen to others and always listen actively.

Be open to understanding and accepting different people's perceptions.

Let the scene itself change your perceptions.

Practice being compassionate.

Open to Understanding
and Accepting new Perceptions
(aka Allowing the scene itself
to Change your Perceptions)

Teniece Divya Johnson

Being

Soluble

in multiple situations

Asks
that We, collectively,
need more

Bend
Ease
Sway
Give

Forgiveness
Gentle
Pull
Mix
Stretch
a multi-fabricated
light-weight
Yogic
Blend
Of flexible
Acceptance

Alive

within our
Interpretation

An Active
Invitation to
Expand
Reaching
Wide
Inclusivity

Permission
to be
Malleable

Moving
Flowing
Meshing
Integrating
Orchestrating

Within
the
conversation
Because
at its Root

Listening

Communication
Interpretation

[Investigation
Policing
Protecting
Our People
and our Nation]
It is

Compromise

Compassion
Sensitivity

Balance

Liberty
Justice

And
Solution Making

Conclusions

Our starting point, three years previously, was that the Hostage Negotiation Team was a silo of space in the police department in which applying the "whole person" to the job was perceived as acceptable. However, this silo of space was proving to be equally detrimental for people who were allowed only temporary access to it as for people who were barred from it altogether, because it was only sanctioned in particular, crisis oriented, branded situations. Our pilot project created a new space, for a broad cohort, inviting people from diverse walks of life together, to engage with the question of applied emotional competence in ways that applied in both daily life and crisis situations.

Time and again, I would hear that the character of the police department was one in which individuals "couldn't feel like people." I would also hear that whenever officers were offered sessions from psychologists or therapists, no one would show up. The perception of engaging with your mental or emotional life was something that itself was silo-ed. One big "ask" of this project, as I heard it, was to create something that was an integrated training, that provided practical skills, incorporated an influential and powerful "Police voice," and also engaged the whole person in a way that the learning arc would override task specific application. We were trying to impact the culture of policing from the position of a human in community.

What did participants take away from this project? I know that they felt like they had been a part of a community of people. I know that this community was comprised of people that many of the participants would normally view as really very different from themselves. I know that they felt like they had gone on a journey of self-reflection and personal growth. I know that many of them would be very averse to engaging with these processes in other contexts. I know that many of the officers felt consistently burnt out and isolated.

I know they had now experienced a "Police Training" that offered them opportunities that counteracted these feelings.

How does this challenge get integrated into formal police training? In the past few years, there have been many initiatives that have begun to emerge in police academies and continuing police education that are geared toward sensitivity training. While this is a positive step, it still represents a siloed approach to education, and misses some very important aspects of the problem of integrating emotional competence in policing. It does not address issues around weak systemic trust, it does not foster integration of knowledge into the whole person, and it runs the risk of being seen as a tool to apply in rigidly specific instances.

Applying a course of study such as this one to a formal police training would require multiple parties to be open to changing themselves. We would all need not only police officers, but the administration, the communities and the local governments to be open to going on a journey of communal growth together. We do learn this lesson as children: we do what we see, not what we're told. Why should we expect police officers to change the way they act and react in high-stakes situations if we're not open to going on a journey of transformation ourselves?

The course of study we have developed offers a small-scale model for initiating a cultural shift that integrates practical policing tools with a personalized understanding of difference, perspective and communication in crisis. It could be applied within communities as well as within various police agencies. We welcome any interest from those who are really committed to finding a new way to work together. Our police do not need to be separate from ourselves if we can together make a shift to see their role as dynamic, as our skin is to the health and regulation of our bodies.

All eye Seeing

Teniece Divya Johnson

All eye Seeing
Void of judging a book by its cover
Investigating to discover
the P.O.V of the other

Balance
In life is maintained
through seeing yourself
And those you love
In the eyes of strangers

An empathy
that dissolves distance
Turning each woman, man and child
Into that of your neighbor
mother, brother or friend

All eye Seeing
Void of judging a book or person by their cover
Actively seeking to discover
The P.O.V. of the other

Allowing you to serve
and protect all under the sun from danger
Void of prejudgment,
Open hearted as you step up to the table
Bringing all of yourself, all your senses
Curious, willing, and able
All eye Seeing
Blind folded like Lady Justice

Committed to a making a better city like Dare Devil
Marvel in the revel of a positive perspective

All eye Seeing
Void of judging a book or person by their cover
Actively seeking to discover
The P.O.V. of the other

⚝ VI ⚝

Collaborative Project Design

This project brought together individuals from law enforcement, crisis management, sociology, medicine, psychology, performance poetry, and socially engaged art. This rich palette of collaborators allowed us to build a project that defied definition, setting a stage on which participants could feel like they were welcome to join the table as co-creators. At the same time as this cross-disciplinary collaboration provided such deep resources, it also challenged the designers. These challenges are worth exploring briefly: they relate directly to the journey and the findings of the project as a whole.

The same fixed perspective we saw in the participants is present in everyone, and at several points in this project there was internal skepticism to overcome, either amongst collaborators or within organizations that they represented. When these roadblocks occur, it can stymie a project's momentum and sometimes can color the outcomes. Part of my job as a Social Practice artist is to attempt to be aware of this and to gently but consistently hold open a space of creativity when obstacles arise that could shut it down. The best way I know to do this is to model the practice of checking your ego at the door, in the service of a greater cause. I'm sure I don't always succeed, but I do try and try and try again.

As you read the writings throughout this book, you can also read in them the authors' own "given circumstances." These are visible in all of our writings, and provide a fascinating context for understanding the different stakeholders who worked on making this experimental art-in-social-practice project possible. You can see the assumptions that are really "sticky" within the comprehension of what the project's aims were, even at the end of the project, and you can draw conclusions about how those "sticky" assumptions can color the nature of the cross-disciplinary collaboration.

I think the best case-scenario is when participants contributing to project design can see themselves as equals to the project participants, and as going on a learning and development journey along the way. Barriers to this deep engagement include perceived time constraints, heavy role identification (what is and isn't my job), status perception, and basic valuing of the impact of the process at the start of the project. And yet there is not likely to be any way to get such a project off the ground without engaging very different kinds of people, with very different expectations as to what the project will be. In other words, a project like this one doesn't just happen. Flexibility as well as commitment are required on all sides.

Learning from this process should therefore impact people interested in collaborative project design, as well as people interested in Emotional Competence in Policing. Learning to be open, active listeners is a challenge for everyone, particularly when doing so from an "on the job" role. One challenge to everyone reading this book should be a personal one: How can I work with others, using the skill of Compassion as my guiding principle? How can I integrate this tool into the foundations of my professional practice?

This challenge is steep. And it is one that we must model, if others are to join in work of this kind. The following sections discuss the opening expectations, the strategic hopes, and the needed adjustments for several of the project's key colleagues.

❧ VII ❧

The Evaluation of a Multidisciplinary Approach to
Emotional Competence Training: Process and Challenges

Georgia Winters & Elizabeth L. Jeglic

Psychologists have been involved with police training for the past several decades. A great deal of police work consists of dealing with "EDPs" — Emotionally Disturbed Persons — an area about which psychologists have expertise. Traditionally, police-psychology collaborations have involved both didactic and experiential portions. Psychologists first explain the symptoms and presentation of individuals suffering various mental disorders, such as anxiety, depression, schizophrenia and borderline personality disorder, to officers. Then, psychologists guide the police officers through various role-playing scenarios on how to work with individuals experiencing mental health crises in a safe and effective manner.

In order to deal with these types of situations successfully, it is important for police officers to recognize their own emotions and those of the individuals they are dealing with — this is what is known as emotional competence. However, emotional competence may be difficult to teach, given the complex nature of understanding emotions. Some feel that this is an innate ability, while others suggest that it is something that can be learned. Assuming that emotional competence is a skill that can be taught, then the question becomes — how does one measure this?

This is precisely the task that we were asked to do. When we joined the project, the program was already developed — which can pose a challenge for program evaluators. Often times, those evaluating the program are involved in the initial design in order to help identify the constructs being taught and how to operationalize and measure the constructs. This program, however, was unique, as it was a collaboration between theater and policing – one of the first of its kind that we are aware of. The collaboration between theater, policing, and psychology was an interesting one. Individuals in these fields attend to the world through different lenses and communicate using different languages. We were faced with several challenges as we learned to speak one another's language. The first challenge we faced was how to define the construct of emotional competence.

In psychology we rely on tests and standardized measures — and in particular, thorough self-report questionnaires. Thus, we first determined the constructs we wanted assessed, such as self-monitoring, perspective taking, personality plasticity, self-esteem, self-regulation, self-compassion, mindfulness, empathy, and autonomy. We then were tasked with finding questionnaire measures to assess these constructs that had been utilized in past research. However, when constructs become less tangible, measuring them becomes much harder. Thus, the constructs become what the questionnaires measure. Not all questionnaires are created equally, and while we may have found measures of these constructs — many of them lacked rigorous scrutiny as to their psychometric properties — such as reliability and validity. In this case, the construct validity would be particularly important — does the questionnaire measure what it says it will be measure? Since many of the questionnaires lacked evidence of strong construct validity, we were left assuming the measures targeted areas related to emotional competence.

Once we decided upon a list of constructs and corresponding questionnaires, we needed to develop an assessment strategy. One of the most common types of designs for program evaluation when teaching new skills is a pre/post design. Using this design, we administer the questionnaires before, and again after the training, to see if there is a change in the measures. The degree to which those measures change from the beginning to the end of the course would in theory reflect the degree to which the trainees "learned" those skills. This strategy, however, is not the ideal way to assess skill acquisition, as we would ideally want to examine the ecological validity and the degree to which the course impacted real world behaviors. This strategy itself comes with a new set of challenges – what behaviors would one expect to see in the field if someone was emotionally competent? Given that in essence this was a pilot test of the training, we decided upon the pre/post design, followed by a questionnaire at the completion of the course to assess participant satisfaction. While in psychology we do not consider satisfaction to be sufficient to determine if a program has achieved its goals, it is important to assess stakeholder buy-in, and participant satisfaction is considered one of those metrics.

Once we received ethics approval from the University ethics committee to administer these questionnaires to participants, the next step was the actual implementation of the evaluative strategy. This is where we once again had a challenge and a clash of disciplinary cultures. As mentioned — in psychology we rely heavily on questionnaires. Much of our research involves studies where we give individuals dozens and even hundreds of questions. While we note participant fatigue as a possible limitation of this methodology, we do not feel that it significantly impacts the overall findings of the study. For this program evaluation, there were about 200 individual questions, which is not considered particularly onerous in psychology studies, and we anticipated that they would take the participants approximately 20 minutes to complete. We were then quite surprised to hear that it took some participants over one hour and that there were complaints about the number of questions. We took this to represent a cultural difference between disciplines. We hypothesize that perhaps the program evaluation aspect of the training was seen as a separate task, not as part of the program itself, making the questionnaire cumbersome. Alternatively, it could mean that indeed there were too many questions — and thus we may need to reconceptualize how we assess change in future studies.

When we initially proposed the evaluative strategy, we also discussed doing some more thematic analyses of the learning process. As the trainees were required to complete various experiential exercises, we had hoped that they would write about their experiences and then we could analyze these writings for themes that related to the constructs that these experimental exercises were trying to teach. However, due to time restraints the students did not write about their experiences consistently, and thus we could not evaluate this aspect of the program. Often times in program evaluation pilot studies, there may be unforeseen barriers that arise through the course of program implementation that limit the evaluative process.

At the conclusion of the program, we administered the post-training questionnaires, which were identical to the ones administered at the start of the program. These were again met with some resistance from the participants, leading to some participants declining to take the questionnaires. In addition to the post course questionnaires, we also administered the satisfaction questionnaire at this time. When we analyzed the results we found no change in the pre/post questionnaire measures. However, the trainees all reported satisfaction with the program — with the only negative being the length of the questionnaires!

This is the first time for us that a program evaluation was viewed so negatively by the participants, and it led us to question why. We also questioned why we did not find any changes in the constructs we were measuring. We came up with a few possible explanations.

The first, and most likely explanation, was that the constructs being taught were not the constructs we were measuring — therefore, it may have been inevitable that we saw no changes. It is possible that we did not define the construct of emotional competence well and, thus, our measures were not accurately targeting what the training sought to teach. It is also possible that the construct was well defined, but that our measures were not valid. It may also be that the participants were not engaged in the process, leading to their responses not accurately reflecting their feelings and perceptions. Given the high level of overall engagement and satisfaction with the program, it is likely that the trainees did benefit from the experiential methods — yet the only way to determine this would be to examine their skills in the field. For us, this means going back to the drawing board, with input from our collaborators, in order to re-evaluate what we are seeking to measure, and how!

⊰ VIII ⊱

Working with a Truly Interdisciplinary Team

Chris Honeyman and Maria R. Volpe

In the Prologue, we referred to our decades of collaboration as the backdrop for this project. Yet most collaborating teams never reach the kind of conceptual breadth you see here. And that's for good reason: Regardless of the degree of social benefit that might result, truly interdisciplinary work is far from easy to do. There have to be individual reasons — even if not exactly the *same* reasons — for all members of such a team to enter into (and stay with!) the collaboration.

Helping prospective team members identify and develop those motivations within themselves, however, is part of the work of our own field of negotiation (along with its allied fields). This particular collaboration was an outlier, at the high end of diversity among all of our joint and individual projects over the years; we think an account of "the mechanics" might be useful to record, particularly for any reader who might contemplate a similar effort in and around his or her own field in the future. So we'll describe the history here.

One of our earlier collaborations in particular became pivotal to all the other collaborative undertakings here. Because the unique team we assembled could be considered counterintuitive in makeup, we will briefly explain how that progenitor came about. In 2001, along with Professor Sandra Cheldelin of George Mason University, Chris and Maria submitted a proposal to the William and Flora Hewlett Foundation, at that time the field's main funder of new research and idea-building. We suggested that its next convening of the 19 so-called Hewlett Theory Centers in Conflict Resolution focus on a problem Chris had identified in his then current (and Hewlett-funded) project, known as Theory to Practice: the lack of effective feedback *from* practice experience *into* research and theory-building.

Maria and Sandra were the directors of two of the Hewlett-funded Theory Centers (Maria, of the CUNY Dispute Resolution Center at John Jay College; Sandra, of the Institute for Conflict Analysis and Resolution, George Mason University — since upgraded to a full-blown School, and now therefore known as S-CAR). The three, with copious help from Hewlett's then program officer Melanie Greenberg, spearheaded and organized the 2002 Theory Centers conference, held at John Jay College. This meeting had a radically different design from any of its predecessors. This became pivotal to what followed.

The two-day-plus meeting of Hewlett-funded scholars and invited conflict resolution colleagues was envisioned to center around three plenary discussions. By the time the planning was well under way, life in New York City was deeply affected by the September 11, 2001 attacks on the World Trade Center. The subsequent discussions and eventual design of the conference reflected this. Accordingly, one of the three plenary sessions featured the best part of a dozen religious leaders, from an equal variety of walks of faith, discussing with a spirited "working audience" of 100 academics their shared and different views of conflict — and its management within their separate faiths and congregations. Another equally noteworthy session, held courtesy of the United Nations at its headquarters in New York City, featured academic interrogation of a UN assistant secretary-general, ambassadors and other high-level diplomats, by scholars selected from among the attendees.

Yet, remarkable as these discussions were, the hands-down most powerful of the three sessions to the group overall was neither of these two. Instead, what really "grabbed" the scholars was a session in which, at our request, four hostage negotiators agreed to be questioned in detail regarding their work on the front lines of conflict intervention — first by two scholars we had selected, and then by the whole group.

The willingness of two successive retired commanders of the already-famous Hostage Negotiation Team of the New York City Police Department, then as now considered the worldwide model for its type of unit, was the direct result of Maria's many years of work with the team, as a colleague at the College and particularly as one of the team's trainers.

Because of that background as well as through Chris's many cases serving as a mediator or arbitrator between police forces and police unions, we were well aware of the "closed shop" world of the police. So we were delighted when Bob Louden and Hugh McGowan, as retirees, were willing to talk about the nuts and bolts of their work, as well as the team's values, its preconceptions, and some of its administrative challenges.

Because the team — which as noted above prides itself on being the only named *team*, in a department of approximately 35,000 uniformed officers that is replete with offices, bureaus, divisions and every other type of administrative unit — must operate within a large bureaucratic context, we were pleasantly surprised to hear that the team's then newly-appointed commander, Jack Cambria, was also willing to join the discussion. The enthusiasm and openness for this plenary session spilled over to another law enforcement agency entirely, so we were able to include a fourth panelist, a hostage negotiator at the FBI, Richard DeFilippo.

Following the conference, Chris, Maria, Sandra and Melanie edited two special issues of Harvard's *Negotiation Journal*. Among the articles was one devoted to the presentations made by the four hostage negotiators. (See Cambria et al 2002.) We have been working with Jack ever since that conference. Among the other collaborative efforts have been chapters co-authored by Jack in four different books edited by Chris, including Chris's and Andrea Schneider's *The*

Negotiator's Fieldbook (American Bar Association 2006) and its replacement, *The Negotiator's Desk Reference* (DRI Press 2017), and *Negotiation Essentials for Lawyers* (ABA 2019.) In short, this has been a rich and productive partnership over a number of years and specific subjects.

Along the way, we had often discussed a training-related topic that was of high interest to Jack. New York City's police department, as noted above, was the originator of a specialized kind of police unit in 1973, now found across the world, of officers with the assignment, skills, experience and training to handle without violence some of the most difficult negotiations known to humankind, between the police and a hostage taker. Knowledge and skills aplenty have been developed for this purpose. The team has amassed a distinguished record.

Yet, a well-known fact is that a trained hostage negotiator is almost never the first responder to the scene of a hostage-taking, a barricaded situation, a threatened suicide, or another incident calling for serious negotiation skills to avert something worse. The City is simply too vast. Even with 100-plus members of the team, when they are spread over many shifts and five boroughs, the chance that one of them can be on the scene before someone else can do something inappropriate, perhaps even fatal, approaches the infinitesimal. A lot can happen before the hostage team members can assemble and respond. The recruits' six month police academy curriculum limits the amount of training hours that can be dedicated to teaching hostage negotiation principles. This had defeated all of Jack's (and his predecessors') arguments to the effect that at least a minimal level of the skills used by experienced hostage negotiators should be taught to every new police officer. (To a certain extent, this situation may now be changing. See Kirschner and Cambria 2017, and Volpe et al 2017. In particular, in the wake of a nationwide string of tragedies best summarized by the placename of Ferguson, Missouri, one resulting course did draw on Jack's experience, and is noted in the two aforementioned book chapters. It was in its design phase concurrently with the planning of the workshop discussed here, however, and followed a very different model. So it is too soon to assess its effects.)

Over years of repeated discussions, the need for more widespread training along the lines of hostage negotiators' training came up many times. By itself, that shared observation counted for little; for a number of years, neither Jack nor Chris could see any practical way of doing anything about it. And by the time the pilot project described in these pages was finally mounted, in 2015, it might appear to the reader that the appalling series of stories from around the US represented by names such as Eric Garner (New York City); Michael Brown (Ferguson, Missouri); Trayvon Martin (Sanford, Florida) and Freddie Gray (Baltimore, Maryland) must have been at the heart of our effort. But while these developments increased our determination, they were not its origin.

The heart of our effort lies instead in the 2007 suicide of an active member of the Hostage Negotiation Team of the New York City Police Department. In a real sense, both our pilot project and this book are dedicated to Detective Lydia Martinez: Her death forced us to recognize both how difficult it was to really know another person's emotional state, and how essential it was to at least try to do something constructive about that.

Chris describes Lydia — an accomplished NYPD hostage negotiator — as the most empathetic human being he has ever encountered. His reaction to her death, like Maria's, was one of shock. But Jack knew her best, and his reaction went beyond shock into something very like denial. By the time Jack was able to write his best tribute to Lydia, several years had elapsed. That tribute became a chapter (see Cambria 2010) in a book Jack describes as "the Bible" of crisis negotiation training. But even with this impetus, it was years before any kind of opportunity, even on an experimental level, presented itself to us. That was a result of a quite different collaboration.

Over roughly the same period of time, scholarship and experiments on the apparently unrelated topic of the use of the arts in conflict management had been growing. One of the earliest inquiries in this line of thinking, as it happened, was conducted by University of British Columbia law professor Michelle LeBaron, in partnership with Chris, in the mid-2000s. It investigated the local culture of Vancouver, which has long used the arts in assessing, understanding, and helping to resolve public conflicts. Their first publication (LeBaron and Honeyman 2006) served as impetus for a larger program by LeBaron, which has now produced distinguished works of multiple kinds. One focus has been on the relationship between willingness to rethink one's stand in a conflict and *physical movement*, particularly dance. Investigating this proposition led to a workshop in Saas Fee, Switzerland in 2010, to which LeBaron invited, among others, Chris — and a theater artist with a deeply social practice named Rachel Parish. Rachel and Chris ended up writing a chapter jointly (Honeyman and Parish 2013) for the book about dance, movement, nonverbal communication and conflict management which LeBaron co-edited as a result of the workshop (LeBaron, MacLeod and Acland 2013.) That book, in an illustration of increasing acceptance of an unorthodox subject in very orthodox quarters, was published in 2013 by the American Bar Association.

2013 also represented the conclusion of a related line of inquiry, one that influenced this project in many ways, in which Chris, with James R. Coben and others, organized and ran the five-year Rethinking Negotiation Teaching project. Among other innovations, that project encouraged fresh thinking about how to redesign specific trainings so that each one would address more closely the kinds of people taking it (Lewicki and Schneider 2010); how to "teach" people who don't normally see themselves as students at all (Blanchot et al 2013; cf. Kirschner and Cambria 2017); how to make the learning of hostage negotiators more broadly available (Volpe and Cambria 2009); and how ideas from theater might relate to uniformed officers who start out far from comfortable with them (Lira and Parish 2013). All of these concepts, as well as broader assessments of the whole sweep of new thinking about negotiation teaching (Fox and Press 2013) and of the role of reputation in every kind of negotiation (Tinsley, Cambria and Schneider 2006, 2017) pervaded our group's thinking throughout this venture.

But by the time the projects noted above were complete, the collaboration discussed in this volume was already off and running. When Chris learned that Rachel, for family reasons, was about to set up a branch of her London theater company in New York for a three-year period, he began to wonder whether Rachel's theater skills and practices might provide a way to approach the obvious-but-unfulfilled need for more effective training of new police officers in the skills of negotiation. As noted above, the possibility also offered the first opening Chris had seen toward a meaningful response to the tragic death by her own hand of an extraordinary member of the Hostage Negotiation Team, Lydia Martinez.

As detailed by Rachel above, the discussion began without a clear idea of what a program might look like. But over two years of engagement and discussion, Jack, Rachel, Maria and Chris formed a perspective that promised to edge free from some of the real and perceived obstacles (institutional, law enforcement, and even scholarly) towards addressing these longstanding issues, and to use the tools that arts-led collaborative practice had to offer. We ultimately agreed that it was best to frame the program we would develop as an arts-based one. Rachel and Jack then proceeded to develop the specific experimental, multi-session workshop detailed in the core of this text.

We also realized that since we were working within an academic context — one where a generous grant was received from Dan and Joanna Rose, pillars of the New York philanthropic community, to support Rachel's and Jack's work — it would be beneficial to incorporate as solid a scholarly assessment of the initiative as the circumstances would permit. To this effect, yet another of our long-standing collaborations became invoked. Chris had first encountered Elizabeth Jeglic, a John Jay colleague of Maria's, in the mid-2000s, when her presentation to a Hostage Negotiation Team training that he was allowed to sit in on practically "knocked him out of his seat." It concerned rates and types of mental illness in society. The heavily-researched numbers exceeded by an order of magnitude what he had imagined.

This encounter resulted, first, in a chapter on "Negotiating with Disordered People" by Elizabeth and Alexander Jeglic in the 2006 *Negotiator's Fieldbook* (now updated as "Mental Health Challenges at the Table" for Honeyman and Schneider 2017.) It also provided the opening for a continuing collaboration. When the present project was ready for that, the resulting discussion, and a significant independent effort, provided the team with the psychological assessments discussed above by Georgia Winters and Elizabeth Jeglic.

As Rachel delicately notes at the head of this section of the book, getting a team of such talented but distinctly different individuals together, and even more, keeping it together till it "produces" is not easy. But it is essential to our shared view of what our field needs, and will continue to need if it is to remain vital. (The risks of *not* making this kind of effort are outlined in a special 19-article issue on "Capitulation to the Routine" in the *Penn State Law Review*, Vol. 108/1, 2003, including Chris's introduction by that title.)

We don't think our own field is alone in needing some new thinking that in turn demands new combinations of skills. And we are far from the only people whose encounters, over years, develop a truly rich array of possible collaborators for some future effort. We hope this sharing of the mechanics of our pilot project will help inspire readers who have been holding the seed of an apparently impossible idea, toward a new round of mulling: Who might be well-positioned, and motivated for their own reasons, to become part of a collaborative venture to help you first brainstorm, and then work on, the previously unimaginable?

Epilogue: Lydia Martinez, Compassion, and Emotional Competence in Policing

Daniel L. Shapiro

Imagine you are called in to negotiate a hostage situation: A man has barricaded himself and his five year old son in their home and threatens to kill the boy unless his ex-wife grants him full custody rights. You stand on the other side of the door, anxious that one wrong move could turn this whole situation into a bloodbath. At this critical moment, your most powerful tool of influence is not a gun but your ability to emotionally connect with the aggrieved father. But how do you do that as your heart races and the father rants?

Emotional competence is critical to effective hostage negotiation. It can mean the difference between cooperation and crisis, life and death. But it is also essential for police officers more broadly: even at junior levels they routinely encounter people who are under great stress. And at the extreme, a trained hostage negotiator is rarely the first responder to an emergent scene. The curriculum you are now reading presents essential insights to turn emotional competence from abstract theory into a concrete set of frameworks and tools.

I came to see the importance of emotional competence within law enforcement through collaboration with the New York Police Department's renowned Hostage Negotiation Team. More than a decade ago, I received an unexpected email from negotiation consultant Chris Honeyman asking whether I wanted to participate in the NYPD's premier hostage negotiation training program. Chris had negotiated permission for a few academics to join in, and I jumped at the opportunity.

The training program was led by Lt. Jack Cambria, distinguished Commanding Officer of the NYPD's Hostage Negotiation Team (2001-2015). The moment we met, he greeted me with a warm smile, firm handshake, and his trademark impeccable character, and for the next five days, I learned from him and his team about the tools of the trade. A big wooden door sat at the front of the room, and we role played crisis situations with police officers acting as hostage negotiators on one side of the door and professional actors playing hostage takers on the other.

I was captivated by the negotiation skill of Lt. Cambria and his close colleague Detective Lydia Martinez, who each maintained laser-like focus on building emotional connection with the hostage taker on the other side of the door. Nothing could shake their focus: The aggrieved party would curse, disparage them, and threaten violence, and they each responded with strength, equanimity, and compassion — to the point that the door between them and the hostage taker seemed to disappear.

Some people might label the skill of Lt. Cambria and Lydia Martinez as "empathy," but it was so much more. Their egos disappeared as they attuned to the hostage taker's emotional world. While an outside observer might judge the perpetrator as "crazy," they sought to discover the logic in that person's seemingly irrational behavior.

More recently, I received another unexpected communication, this time from Lt. Jack Cambria, whose usually strong voice quivered as he told me that Lydia had taken her own life. She was family to him and a role model for me. I was heartbroken. To this day, I do not know the details of how it happened or why, but I have come to realize that true connection is an energy-intensive activity. Lydia had a rare gift for connecting with even the most anguished soul, to the extent that it may have drained the energy from her own.

So why this book? Because the tools and activities within these pages can help young police officers and officers-in-training learn something of how hostage negotiators attune to their own emotional world and that of the hostage taker. Lydia was blessed with an unusual ability to connect, and she was able to save the lives of countless individuals through her selfless belief in the human spirit. This book reveals some of the tools that Lydia intuitively applied to connect with others.

I wish I could have just one more conversation with Lydia, to let her know the extent to which she emotionally touched the lives of so many people, mine included. This book speaks to the heart of Detective Martinez's gift, offering a powerful program to bring people dealing with a crisis one step closer to each other, so that both justice and humanity can flourish.

Further Reading

Alexander, N. and LeBaron, M. (2017) Aesthetics in Negotiation: Part One—Four Elements. In *The Negotiator's Desk Reference*, edited by C. Honeyman and A.K. Schneider. St: Paul: DRI Press.

Blanchot, E., Ebner, N., Honeyman, C., Kaufman, S. and Parish, R. (2013) The Education of Non-Students. In *Educating Negotiators for a Connected World*, edited by C. Honeyman, J. Coben, and A. W-M. Lee. St. Paul: DRI Press.

Cambria, J., De Filippo, R., Louden, R. and McGowan, H. (2002) Negotiation Under Extreme Pressure: The Mouth Marines and the Hostage Takers. *Negotiation Journal*, Vol 18/4

Cambria, J. (2010) Coping with the Suicide of a Team Member. In *Crisis Negotiations: Managing Critical Incidents and Hostage Situations in Law Enforcement and Corrections*, edited by M. McMains and W. Mullins. 4th Edition. Routledge

Fox, K. and Press, S. (2013) Venturing Home: Implementing Lessons from the Rethinking Negotiation Teaching Project. In *Educating Negotiators for a Connected World*, edited by C. Honeyman, J. Coben, and A. W-M. Lee. St. Paul: DRI Press.

Honeyman, C. and Parish, R. (2013) Choreography of Negotiation: Movement in Three Acts. In *Choreography of Resolution: Conflict, Movement and Neuroscience*, edited by M. LeBaron, C. MacLeod and A. F. Acland. Washington, DC: American Bar Association.

Jeglic, E. and Jeglic., A. (2006) Negotiating with Disordered People. In *The Negotiator's Fieldbook*, edited by A.K. Schneider and C. Honeyman. Washington, DC: American Bar Association.

Jeglic, E. and Jeglic., A. (2017) Mental Health Challenges at the Table. In *The Negotiator's Desk Reference*, edited by C. Honeyman and A.K. Schneider. St: Paul: DRI Press.

Jendresen, C. (2017) Creativity and Flexibility in the Brain. In *The Negotiator's Desk Reference*, edited by C. Honeyman and A.K. Schneider. St: Paul: DRI Press.

Kirschner, S.M. and Cambria, J. (2017) Training a Captive Audience. In *The Negotiator's Desk Reference*, edited by C. Honeyman and A.K. Schneider. St: Paul: DRI Press.

LeBaron, M. and Honeyman, C. (2006) Using the Creative Arts. In *The Negotiator's Fieldbook*, edited by A.K. Schneider and C. Honeyman. Washington, DC: American Bar Association.

LeBaron, M. and Alexander, N. (2017) Aesthetics in Negotiation: Part Two—the Uses of Alchemy. In *The Negotiator's Desk Reference*, edited by C. Honeyman and A.K. Schneider. St: Paul: DRI Press.

LeBaron, M., MacLeod, C. and Acland, A.F. (2013) *Choreography of Resolution: Conflict, Movement and Neuroscience.* Washington, DC: American Bar Association.

Lewicki, R. and Schneider, A.K. (2010) Instructors Heed the Who: Designing Negotiation Training with the Learner in Mind. In *Venturing Beyond the Classroom*, edited by C. Honeyman, J.R. Coben and G. De Palo. St: Paul: DRI Press.

Lira, L.L. and Parish, R. (2013) Making it Up as You Go: Educating Military and Theater Practitioners in "Design". In *Educating Negotiators for a Connected World*, edited by C. Honeyman, J. Coben, and A. W-M. Lee. St. Paul: DRI Press.

Maslach, C., Jackson, S.E., Leiter, M.P. (1996, 2016) *Maslach Burnout Inventory Manual* (Fourth Edition). Menlo Park, CA: Mind Garden, Inc.

O'Shea, J. (2017) Caring for People on the Edge: Emergency Medicine, Negotiation and the Science of Compassion. In *The Negotiator's Desk Reference*, edited by C. Honeyman and A.K. Schneider. St: Paul: DRI Press.

Tinsley, C.H., Cambria, J., and Schneider, A.K. (2017) Reputation in Negotiation. In *The Negotiator's Desk Reference*, edited by C. Honeyman and A.K. Schneider. St: Paul: St. Paul: DRI Press.

Vecchi, G.M., Van Hasselt, V.B. and Romano, S.J. (2005) Crisis (Hostage) Negotiation: Current Strategies and Issues in High-Risk Conflict Resolution. *Aggression and Violent Behavior* 10: 533–551.

Volpe, M. and Cambria, J. (2009) Negotiation Nimbleness When Cultural Differences are Unidentified. In *Rethinking Negotiation Teaching*, edited by C. Honeyman, J. Coben, and G. De Palo. St. Paul: DRI Press.

Volpe, M., Cambria, J., McGowan, H. and Honeyman, C. (2017) Negotiating with the Unknown. In *The Negotiator's Desk Reference*, edited by C. Honeyman and A.K. Schneider. St: Paul: DRI Press.

Student Reactions to the Experimental Course

In contrast to today's charged environment, *The Other Side of the Door* offers a shining example of how policing should be done: with insight, empathy and compassion. This book offers more than a vision: it provides specific examples borne from years of on-the-job experience in NYC's challenging hostage negotiation environment, where applying these principles saved lives. Indeed, the applications of this book and course go beyond policing. It is highly recommended reading for anyone with authority and discretion about how to conduct themselves with staff or customers, as well as members of a greater community. I very much appreciated being part of this extraordinary project.

Alex Yaroslavsky

As an officer on the streets of New York City you have to be ready for anything. This course and its knowledge add more tools to my tool box for the sometimes not so nice Streets of NYC.

Rich Hornberger

I was thrilled to be able to take part in this project..... After graduating from John Jay, I have been able to use the lessons (from) this project in not only my personal, but also professional life. The project has helped me to reframe my perception of situations which I encounter, looking at the entirety of the situation rather than only at what is right in front of me. Something as simple as taking a step back and observing one's surroundings (what you hear, smell, and see) outside of the immediate situation can provide information which might shape the way I react to a situation.....I am certain that the skills I learned during this project....created a fantastic base for me to build upon.

Alex H. Levitz

It was an honor to be in the Experimental Course concerning negotiation and mood control. As a police officer I need to face different people every day — colleagues, suspects and the many people who need our help. Sometimes it's really stressful and I am on the edge of losing my temper. At that moment, your words in that wonderful course, and the small cards you gave me — which I keep on my desk — remind me to control myself and put my feet into the other's shoes. It really works and always leads to a good result. (The workshop) showed me not only the skills of negotiation and mood control, but the way and attitude I should have in life, to others and to myself.

ZHOU Qinggang
Superintendent of Police
Yunnan Public Security Department, China